NEVER PAY RETAIL FOR COLLEGE

HOW SMART PARENTS FIND THE RIGHT SCHOOL FOR THE RIGHT PRICE

BETH V. WALKER

Founder, Center for College Solutions

NEVER PAY RETAIL FOR COLLEGE

HOW SMART PARENTS FIND THE RIGHT SCHOOL FOR THE RIGHT PRICE

BETH V. WALKER

Founder, Center for College Solutions

Published by Prussian Press

Copyright 2017 © Beth V. Walker

Paperback ISBN: 978-1-61961-533-5
EBook ISBN: 978-1-61961-612-7

Interior design: 3CsBooks.com

DEDICATION

For Mack,

Chisel away, Prussian Prince.

INVITATION TO
CONNECT

Get insights, tips and tools for finding the right college
and always paying less than retail.

NeverPayRetailForCollege.com/newsletter

TABLE OF CONTENTS

INTRODUCTION

If what you thought you knew about college turned out not to be true, when would you want to know? As soon as possible? In time to do something about it?

I'm so glad you've found this book. In these pages, I will share with you the sobering news about higher education as it exists today. To bring you up to speed, you should know that college is more competitive, costly, complicated, and confusing than it was when we walked those hallowed halls of academia. Our relentless and seductive consumer culture has convinced us that college is a product, something with pretty packaging and a list of features a mile long that our kids can't live without. As parents, we're desperate to get the best product we can for our children. We're willing to go into debt and work longer before retiring so our kids can have every opportunity to succeed in this hypercompetitive, global economy.

It's a heavy burden we carry. As a parent, I understand where you're coming from. College is a six-figure endeavor and a large part of the way we prepare our children for success in adult life. No pressure, right? The trouble is that the pressure is overwhelming, and that alone makes it hard to see things clearly. We think we know what we're doing and how we should go about this.

What I've discovered is we're doing it all wrong.

We need to reboot our beliefs and assumptions about college. So much has changed since we went to school. It's time to step back and reframe this thing in a way that allows us to take control of our finances and our kids' futures.

College is a project, not a product.

College is a multi-year project that is 10 times more expensive than the average kitchen remodel. But like a remodel, it takes planning to pull it off successfully: an investment of time, energy, and money in advance. No one person can complete the entire project. We need a team of experts and someone who sees the BIG picture and pays attention to the details and the schedule to bring the project in on time and on budget.

Who's running your six-figure project called college? You? Your student? How are decisions being made about who's doing what, when and how? And is everybody clear on the why behind all this activity, stress and money?

Conventional wisdom tells us to accept the recommendations of magazines and school counselors—sources that are not picking up the check and don't have skin in *our* game. The advice offered is generic, and the process they recommend is outdated. They aren't bad people, but they're focused on college for all kids, not our kid.

I'm a mom on a mission. I collaborate with other moms and dads to create better futures—for their kids and for themselves. And it all centers around the project called "college."

Fourteen years ago, my professional life and my personal life collided with the birth of my son, Mack. I was a financial planner long before I was a mom. But when Mack was born, I took eight weeks off to be home with him. Between changing diapers and recovering from a cesarean section, I did a geeky financial planner thing. I went to the College Board's college cost calculator and projected the cost of educating our little bundle of joy.

I wasn't prepared for what the calculator was telling me. At first, I thought sleep deprivation had impaired my brain. The number before me couldn't possibly be correct. There was no way it was going to cost us more than $250,000 to put our little guy through college.

Fast forward to today, and I find myself doing for other families what I'm doing for my own household: making sure we never pay retail for college.

As a mother, I understand the emotional, nail-biting aspects of this challenge. This six-figure project is loaded with emotion and the stress that comes from information overwhelm, not knowing who to trust, and the need to *get this right*. As a college fiduciary, I understand the pragmatic, financial components of the whole equation and can guide you through, step by step.

A fiduciary is someone who acts, at all times, in the family's best interest and for their sole benefit. As a college fiduciary, I have the expertise and know-how that comes from going through the process repeatedly. I provide information, recommendations, and support for the families I serve to guide them in meeting their goals and objectives for higher education. I exercise care in making recommendations, always asking, *would I do what I'm suggesting?* My loyalty is to the family, so I avoid conflicts that come from serving more than one master.

My position as a fiduciary affords me the perspective to see the big picture and the familiarity to see things clearly. You see, once we reframe college by breaking it into manageable parts and assigning responsibility where it belongs, we discover it's more straightforward, less stressful, and delivers a much better outcome for everyone involved.

I've seen the stress that college creates. Parents wonder about paying for college, and teenagers feel anxious because everyone is asking them where they're going and what they will study. Often, no one knows how to answer the questions they're being asked.

We can put an end to the unanswered questions. Parents can know exactly how much they can afford to invest in launching their kids without jeopardizing retirement, and students can set foot on campus with a sense of purpose and a clearly defined game plan. They can get a four-year degree in four years and put themselves on a path toward a satisfying and meaningful future. We can't eliminate the stress—as parents, we will always worry—but we can transform overwhelming anxiety into healthy, motivating energy that helps you and your student take action to move toward your goals. We can do this so much better and for a lot less money.

What I've come to understand—with lots of effort and education; the guidance of admissions counselors, financial aid experts, scholarship gurus, talented financial advisers; and the patience and understanding of some very determined parents— is that college is the mother of all project plans, and we need to approach it like a six-figure kitchen remodel.

Just like a kitchen remodel requires a plumber, an electrician, granite counter top experts, and appliance installers, the college project requires a variety of seasoned subcontractors too. I've spent the last 14 years figuring out who those experts are, which tools and techniques make a difference, who needs to do what— and when—so the college project can come in on time and on budget.

I'm an experienced project manager that approaches the project called college with the heart of a mother and the mind of a financial planner. And I've cultivated a roster of smart, experienced, like-minded professionals committed to reducing stress and saving families both time and money on their college project.

Before we get started, I want to orient you to what you'll find in *Never Pay Retail for College*. One of the biggest stumbling blocks families encounter in planning for this project is that they don't have a clear idea of who is supposed to do what and when or how it needs to be done. I've structured this book to provide clarity for a successful project. The chapters dealing with the tasks provide information about who is responsible, what they are responsible for, and when it needs to occur. At the end of each chapter, I've included Project Plan Essentials, the important points of focus from the chapter.

This book reflects my experience as a college fiduciary working with families all over the country to make college an affordable reality. Throughout these pages, I share the stories of parents and students who have taught me how this stuff works in the real world. To protect their privacy, I have changed names and details and created composites from those with similar experiences. In doing so, it is my hope that every family can see themselves in the stories I include, but any resemblance to a particular situation or person is coincidental.

In chapter 1, I show you the college landscape as it exists today. We need to understand the good and bad so we can craft a plan based on reality. You'll learn that applying for college has become more complex, competitive, and costly than when we were high school students. You need to know this, but don't be discouraged. I will guide you through the project in the rest of the book to help you avoid the mistakes that families often make.

In chapters 2–5, you'll learn about the student's portion of the project plan: match qualifications to the various colleges, prepare for college admissions, gain self-awareness, and get the right mindset. Parents can support and influence their students, but this is the student's domain. In chapters 6–8, the parents take center stage. Their portion of the project plan includes estimating the family contribution, applying for financial aid, and assessing retirement readiness so they can calculate the available cash flow for college. Then in chapters 9–12, the family comes together to select right-fit colleges, assess scholarship options, compare financial aid awards, and transition successfully to college. In the conclusion, I share my final thoughts about this challenging project, and finally share a long and rich list of resources arranged by chapter topics.

The best way to approach this book and the material in it is to read all the way through so you have a broad understanding of the project before you. Write down any questions and concerns you have as you go. Then read it again focusing on the items that need attention first. Let your student explore the book as well. Everyone needs to understand how this works and what their role is.

My guess is that you picked up this book to find strategies and tactics to reduce your costs, minimize the complexity of this project, and ease your stress. I welcome the opportunity to provide you with experienced project management—saving you both time and money—and look forward to ensuring you never pay retail for college.

CHAPTER ONE

TODAY'S COLLEGE LANDSCAPE

Parents Jeff and Jenny shared their feelings of defeat and embarrassment with me over a chai tea latte and grande mocha at a local Starbucks. They are the modern-day Brady Bunch: a blended family brought together after two divorces, with four kids to put through college. Jeff and Jenny are financially responsible parents, but they sure didn't feel that way. Despite generating more than $200,000 in combined income, they were struggling with credit card debt and constant cash flow stress.

"Every time I turn around, I'm forking out $250 for sports, $100 for a school-related activity, or $300 for a car repair," said Jenny. "Just buying groceries for four kids is enough to break the bank."

Jenny is a teacher. She recently took a second job as a soccer referee every Saturday to supplement their income and pay down the credit card debt that has crept past $30,000. Jeff is an executive for a national company. He has considered becoming an Uber driver during his nonworking hours to generate additional cash flow so they don't fall further behind on the credit cards.

These are responsible, educated, and intelligent parents who are at their wit's end.

With two kids already in college, another one starting in the fall, and the youngest graduating next May, they feel completely overwhelmed with the realities of educating their kids while trying to maintain their current lifestyle. I can assure you, the thought of retiring isn't even on their radar.

Jenny had set aside some money for her kids during her first marriage but has received no child support from her former spouse. Jeff is paying child support that will end once his youngest child turns eighteen.

This family has too much month left at the end of their paychecks. Even if each kid takes out student loans, they still must come up with more than their mortgage payment each month to pay for college and pay their credit card debt on top of that. They are spent—financially and emotionally.

We talked for an hour about the reality of their current financial situation. I helped them think through how to restructure their debt, find cash flow for college, and continue to fund their current lifestyle, without Jenny giving up every Saturday or Jeff picking up Uber shifts on the weekends.

When Jenny excused herself to use the restroom, Jeff looked at me and said, "I'm embarrassed to be sitting here having this conversation. I can't believe I let it get to this point." As the primary breadwinner, he has been crushed by the seriousness of his family's financial circumstances.

I gently reminded him that he had more than a full-time job and twice as many kids as most parents in America to put through college. My words relieved some of his burden, and the plan the three of us crafted together restored some emotional and financial sanity to their situation.

Unfortunately, Jeff and Jenny's story is not unusual. It's happening in households across the country these days. In my experience, no other financial demand is as emotionally charged and draining as college. As human beings—let alone as parents— we aren't wired to decide about college based on money and logic. Therefore, we don't.

In fact, United Capital, the first and largest Financial Life Management firm, commissioned a study that showed most people make important financial decisions that align with their personal values. *After* they've made spending decisions, people assess the financial consequences of their choices.[1] College becomes an unconscious expression of our value system as parents. The financial realities reveal themselves only in a "morning after" reality check, leaving us wondering how we got into such a mess.

---

[1] William Conroy, "United Capital Studies Clients' Secret Needs and Desires," *Financial Advisor*, April 20, 2015 (http://www.fa-mag.com/ news/united-capital-learn-what-clients-really-want-21431.html).

Parents read that "the cost of college has been rising much faster than the rate of inflation,"[2] but it's hard to put that into context. It's really instructive, though, if we do.

In 1971, Harvard's annual tuition was $2,600. If inflation were the only factor contributing to the increase in costs since then, today's students would pay a bit more than $15,000 per year. Current Harvard students pay more than $47,000 annually—just for tuition. That doesn't include where they sleep (room), what they eat (board), or the necessary textbooks, supplies, and other miscellaneous fees. Or traveling to and from school every year.

I don't mean to pick on Harvard. Full-time tuition at Auburn for a nonresident was $2,585 for the 1985–1986 school year. Now it's $28,040. Don't you wish your 401(k) balance experienced the same compounded annual growth rate of 8.27 percent for decades and never saw a negative market correction?

According to the news agency Bloomberg, college tuition and fees have increased 1,120 percent since it began tracking this information in 1978. Every institution of higher education has taken part in this escalating arms race. Of course, schools promote the fact that they have the most reputable professors, modern and comfortable student housing, a completely wired campus, the best climbing walls and espresso bars, and so forth. They are competing for our hard-earned money. It makes sense that they double down on sexy amenities to attract students that will boost their rankings and pass the costs along to us.

---

[2] Kim Clark, "College Board Says Tuition Rose Faster Than Inflation Again This Year," *Money*, November 4, 2015 (http://time.com/money/4098683/college-board-tuition-cost-rose-inflation-2015/).

The cost of college has accelerated further and faster than any other category of spending we measure while wages have remained constant or declined. In plain English, college consumes more and more of our paychecks, and parents no longer have the luxury of "dealing with it when we get there" like our parents did.

The table below demonstrates how rising tuition rates gradually eat up more of our monthly income each year.

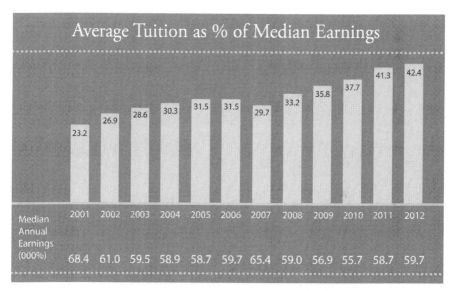

Source: Bureau of Labor Statistics (BLS); Integrated Postsecondary Education Data System (IPEDS)

So why do parents continue to take on this increasingly difficult challenge, often going into debt or agreeing to work much longer than they ever thought they would? Because the only thing more expensive than a college education is *not* having a college education as you can see in the chart below.

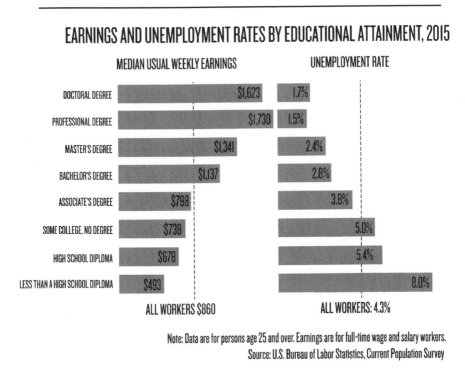

EARNINGS AND UNEMPLOYMENT RATES BY EDUCATIONAL ATTAINMENT, 2015

	MEDIAN USUAL WEEKLY EARNINGS	UNEMPLOYMENT RATE
DOCTORAL DEGREE	$1,623	1.7%
PROFESSIONAL DEGREE	$1,730	1.5%
MASTER'S DEGREE	$1,341	2.4%
BACHELOR'S DEGREE	$1,137	2.8%
ASSOCIATE'S DEGREE	$798	3.8%
SOME COLLEGE, NO DEGREE	$738	5.0%
HIGH SCHOOL DIPLOMA	$678	5.4%
LESS THAN A HIGH SCHOOL DIPLOMA	$493	8.0%
	ALL WORKERS $860	ALL WORKERS: 4.3%

Note: Data are for persons age 25 and over. Earnings are for full-time wage and salary workers.
Source: U.S. Bureau of Labor Statistics, Current Population Survey

We need to realize that college is perhaps the largest unregulated industry in our economy, and it's extremely competitive, meaning colleges compete fiercely with each other to fill their classrooms. Granted, the name brand institutions have the luxury of turning away most students, but hundreds and hundreds of colleges each year scramble to meet their quotas. In this environment, we need to strap on our protective armor and be prepared to do battle with a consumer mentality, not just the heart of a parent.

Aside from the cost, students face unprecedented competition to get into college because too many students apply to too few schools that have recognizable names and effective marketing campaigns. Technology has made it much easier to complete more applications in less time. The Common Application allows students to apply to multiple schools simultaneously with a single click. Three million students graduate from high school every year in the United States, and a little more than two million of them are enrolled in college a few months after graduating. All those kids fill out numerous applications (the most recent data suggest 25 percent of applicants complete seven or more applications for college) and write countless essays to eat lackluster dorm food nine months out of the year. Admissions committees are forced to sift through thousands more applications and must eliminate a far greater number of students than ever before.

Significant increases in enrollment from international students adds to the competition. A *Wall Street Journal* article published in November 2015 reported that one in twenty college students enrolled in US universities comes from outside the United States.[3] Because so many of those students are paying retail for their US education, the appetite for admitting those "full-pay" students continues to grow, eliminating a few more "home team" seats each year.

More students are applying for a finite number of spots in name-brand schools touted by magazines and glossy brochures. Classic supply-and-demand rules indicate this won't work out in favor of most students or their parents. Increasing demand

---

[3] Douglas Belkin, "Foreign Enrollment at U.S. Colleges Sets a Record," *Wall Street Journal*, November 16, 2015 (http://www.wsj.com/articles/foreign-enrollment-at-u-s-colleges-hits-a-record-1447650062).

chasing (what is perceived to be a) limited supply favors the supplier. As the costs and competition increase, families have started to seek ways to make this must-have rite of passage more attainable.

But it's complicated.

Type *college admissions* into Google's search box, and 109,000,000 links will appear on your screen in less than one second; search on *paying for college*, and 216,000,000 suggested resources are at your fingertips. Try *financial aid* or *scholarships*, and again, more than 131,000,000 ideas to ponder await you.

Is it any wonder most families feel overwhelmed and confused about what to do or who to trust? The sheer volume of information and conflicting advice is mind numbing. We'd like to believe the high school our student attends is on top of the college project, proactively preparing our student to navigate the increasingly complex frontier.

As parents, we are on the verge of making a six-figure financial decision. We find ourselves at the mercy of a seventeen-year-old and, unfortunately, their guidance counselor (who is being asked to take on more and more responsibility for mental health and behavioral issues with *zero* continuing education requirements regarding college admissions).

It's not productive to play the blame game or rail against the injustices of this institutionalized waste of time and money; we need to stay focused on finding solutions.

Our parents didn't confront the costs, competition, or complexity that we face in today's college process. Like so many things in today's world, the responsibility for knowing what to do (e.g., buy or lease a car? Make extra payments on the mortgage?

Max out the 401(k) plan or just up to the company match?) and how to do it all falls on our shoulders. Most parents have no formal training in economics or asset allocation or the time value of money. We're so busy juggling full-time jobs, kids' schedules, running our households, and supporting aging and ailing parents that we have almost no time to read the mail in our inbox, let alone the mailbox at the end of the driveway. Forget being a good consumer of financial advice or strategic planning.

We are spinning a lot of plates and can't afford to let any of them drop. We need help. We need to know what to do, when to do it, who should do it, and how to put all the pieces of the puzzle together in a way that works for our unique situation.

As parents, we are about to embark on our personal, financial trek up Mount Everest, and we find ourselves looking around for an experienced Sherpa to guide us on this treacherous ascent. But who can we turn to for that guidance? Where are the grizzled veterans of this journey who can help us avoid the most common pitfalls and danger zones? Who can keep us on a path and give us a fighting chance to get to where we're going, with the least amount of pain and permanent damage?

I've set out to provide a field-tested guide on how to never pay retail for college. This book shares what I've learned over the years and what I'm doing in my own household. This is how I'm approaching my own college project to achieve the best outcome for my family and avoid paying retail.

If you take a few good ideas from what I'm sharing, and if I can help you maintain your sanity during the process, my years of running a nonprofit (my husband's affectionate term for my business) will have been worth it. I've tested everything I can get my hands on to make this process more manageable and found some of the best people in the industry for specialized help.

As I've worked with families over the years, it's clear that certain activities and responsibilities fall into three distinct categories. There are certain elements only the student can or should do; there are also obligations in this project that only the parents should manage. Finally, some components require the student and parents to work together to achieve the best possible outcome. I've organized this book accordingly.

I've learned that much of the stress in the going-to-college project happens when parents insert themselves in areas where the student is the one for the job or when a parent mistakenly assumes the student will tackle tasks they aren't equipped to handle. You wouldn't want the plumber installing the flooring for your kitchen remodel. But by the time a family reaches the point where it makes sense to work together, the whole college conversation has already come off the rails. Parental nagging and teenage avoidance can escalate so that everyone simply wants to get through the whole mess and, hopefully, remain on speaking terms.

College *is* the mother of all project plans.

If ever there was a time to get up to speed on the principles of project management, this is it. The Association of Project Management (APM) defines project management as "an endeavor in which human material and financial resources are organized in a novel way to deliver a unique scope of work of given specification, often within constraints of cost and time to achieve beneficial changes defined by quantitative and qualitative objectives."

Translation: This project is about finding a college that provides your kid with a great education and experience, gets them in and out in four years, and doesn't break the bank.

Most parents aren't Project Management Professionals (PMPs) but are forced into that role to get their kids through college. Think of this book as your field manual. Understand that like any lengthy, multiphase project (back to the kitchen remodel), it requires focus on the *big picture*, attention to detail along the way, a willingness to invest time and money on a smaller scale to save money down the road, and an ability to supervise those aspects of the project that have to be subbed out.

Knowing who needs to do what and when alleviates much of the arguing and anxiety. How we put all of this together is what I call the Never Pay Retail for College™ Success Plan to help smart parents find the right school for the right price.

Never Pay Retail for College™ Success Plan
Find the Right School for the Right Price

Visit www.CenterForCollegeSolutions.com
to download a Success Plan Timeline

This recipe for success is simple and straightforward, but it takes time and attention to execute. In a perfect world, we would digest and take the Success Plan to heart *before our student starts high school*, which would allow for things to unfold in a natural and manageable rhythm. However, it's not too late if our student is already on the verge of college admissions applications. You can accelerate the way you apply the formula, but you'll need to buckle up and put the pedal to the metal.

PROJECT PLAN ESSENTIALS

- College is a project, not a product.

- Thoughtful investments of time and money during the high school years will save us tens of thousands of dollars during the college years.

PART I:

THE STUDENT

Match Qualifications to Colleges

Prep for College Admissions

Gain Self - Awareness

Get the Right Mindset

Every block of stone has a statue inside it and it is the task of the sculptor to discover it.

—MICHELANGELO

The hardest part of being a parent is understanding that we are not the sculptor Michelangelo speaks of. Our children are working on their own block of stone. With the hard-earned wisdom of our years and life experience, it's tempting to wrestle the chisel and hammer from their grasp and "help." But this statue is not ours to sculpt. They must do the work and reveal the underlying masterpiece that is their life.

As a supportive patron of the arts, we can and should encourage our children's efforts—but in helpful ways. In an essay adapted from her new book, *The Gardener and the Carpenter: What the New Science of Child Development Tells Us about the Relationship between Parents and Children*,[4] Dr. Alison Gopnik says we need to view our role as gardeners and create an environment in which our children can flourish.

The student is accountable for matching their qualifications to colleges, applying for college admission, becoming self-aware, and developing a mindset that serves their future. We must *hold them capable* of discovering themselves by stepping back and letting them experience the consequences of their decisions while we're still around to provide a safety net and help them connect the dots in a way that can only come from our years of experience.[5]

What follows is an in-depth look at each of the important components of getting ready for college so that we can prepare fertile soil for their development.

---

[4] Alison Gopnik, "A Manifesto against 'Parenting,'" *Wall Street Journal*, July 8, 2016 (http://www.wsj.com/articles/a-manifesto-against-parenting-1467991745).

[5] For more support in this area, read *Duct Tape Parenting: A Less Is More Approach to Raising Respectful, Responsible, and Resilient Kids* by Vicki Hoefle.

CHAPTER TWO

MATCH
QUALIFICATIONS
TO COLLEGES

When students knock on the doors of colleges, they don't arrive empty-handed. They come bearing their high school transcript, unweighted grade point average (GPA), and standardized test scores. Together, I call these your student's "college capital." Colleges will size up these three components before even thinking about inviting applicants in. Your student's college capital is the foundation of the college project.

The "college capital" your student creates is the by-product of their work in high school. What students do along the way—

the experiences they have, the classes they take, the grades they earn, the life lessons they discover, and so forth—is all wonderful and enriches their lives and the journey. Education and the corresponding credentials matter, but learning matters more. Your student's college capital is a currency only they can trade.

And we can't do it for them.

We can teach them to be capable. We can push them beyond their comfort zone. We can hold them to a higher standard than they've set for themselves and set an example with our words and actions. We can support our kids and provide them with project management tools that allow them to organize, store, and share their research and work. We can subcontract with a coach who specializes in working with students to guide them, hold them accountable, and help them work smarter instead of harder on their elements of the college project. But again, our action in this space is a supporting role: only the student can do those things that will determine where they will be in the pecking order of college admissions.

College fit is relative and based on the student's learning style and temperament. College cost depends largely on parents accepting that theory of relativity. You will pay retail if you insist that your student apply and attend those reach schools that magazines and counselors tout. As parents, we've been sold a bill of goods that this futile and expensive exercise – applying to reach schools - is worthwhile when it's not.

When we buy a house, the purchase price depends on what we can afford and the financing we qualify for. We let the amount of the prequalified mortgage and factors like distance from work and the quality of local schools determine the zip code.

When our student starts driving, we don't drop him off at the car dealer and tell the salesperson to let him buy any car on the lot. Again, we let our cash flow and safety features dictate the range of choices for transportation to find a good fit for our new driver.

So why do we entertain this six-figure financial decision with an open-ended checkbook? Because we don't approach college like other large lifestyle purchases; we lead with our hearts, not our heads, and often pay a price for doing it that way. Shouldn't we understand what our student qualifies for in terms of scholarships, discounts, and financial aid *before we even apply?*

The conventional path—applying to reach, target, and safety schools then attending the most prestigious school that accepts the student—is creating conventional results with harsh consequences that can last years after your student completes their college project. That's a recipe for paying retail.

We need to archive that approach, along with the phonograph, pay phone, and typewriter. That path for getting to and through college worked fine in the past, and we may even feel a bit of nostalgia for the good old days. But the world has changed drastically, and we must look out the windshield, not observe things in the rear view mirror.

There is a better way to play the college game and it all starts with the student.

Parents need to understand how impactful the student's college capital will be on the eventual cost of college and the real options they should consider. The fact is, as parents we can influence those credentials, but we can't control them. They will be the result of the effort the student puts in over the four years of high school, and we must work with the student's credentials when we get there.

The three critical components—unweighted GPA, ACT or SAT test scores, and the high school transcript—should dictate to which colleges our students apply.[6] Later in the book, I will cover the importance of a strategic approach to creating a college list, but the message here is that these three components matter more than anything else. Yes, extracurricular activities are nice. Yes, community service makes for a more rounded person and is good for the soul. But, the real currency, the capital that counts when applying for college, is made up of those three components: grades, test scores, and the strength of the high school curriculum.

John Wooden was a successful coach by any standard. Most basketball enthusiasts admire the "Wizard of Westwood" for masterminding ten National College Athletic Association (NCAA) national championships in a twelve-year period. His remarkable accomplishments as a basketball coach pale in comparison to the value he brings us as parents. His coaching methods are directly applicable to how we can patiently foster an atmosphere that allows our kids to become the best versions of themselves, whatever that turns out to be.

The following excerpts from Coach Wooden's February 2001 TED Talk set the stage for creating a framework for this part of the process:

> I coined my own definition of success, which is, peace of mind attained only through self-satisfaction in knowing you made the effort to do the best of which you're capable. I believe that's true. If you make the effort to do the best of which you're capable, trying to improve the

---

6   National Association for College Admission Counseling, "Factors in the Admission Decision," retrieved October 22, 2016 (http://www.nacacnet.org/studentinfo/articles/Pages/Factors-in-the-Admission-Decision.aspx).

situation that exists for you, I think that's success, and I don't think others can judge that; it's like character and reputation. Your reputation is what you're perceived to be; your character is what you really are. And I think that character is much more important than what you are perceived to be. You'd hope they'd both be good, but they won't necessarily be the same.

That's what really matters: if you make an effort to do the best you can regularly, the results will be about what they should be. Not necessarily what you'd want them to be, but they'll be about what they should; only you will know whether you can do that. And that's what I wanted from them more than anything else. And as time went by, and I learned more about other things, I think it worked a little better, as far as the results. But I wanted the score of a game to be the by-product of these other things and not the end itself. I believe it was one great philosopher who said—no, no—Cervantes. Cervantes said, "The journey is better than the end." And I like that. I think that it is—it's getting there. Sometimes when you get there, there's almost a letdown. But it's the getting there that's the fun.

Not necessarily what you'd want them to be, but they'll be about what they should.

These are brilliant words from a man who was quite successful at getting young people to realize their potential. When it comes to creating college capital, our role is a supporting one.

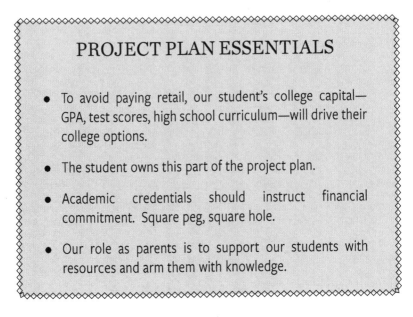

PROJECT PLAN ESSENTIALS

- To avoid paying retail, our student's college capital—GPA, test scores, high school curriculum—will drive their college options.

- The student owns this part of the project plan.

- Academic credentials should instruct financial commitment. Square peg, square hole.

- Our role as parents is to support our students with resources and arm them with knowledge.

CHAPTER THREE

PREP for COLLEGE ADMISSIONS

W hen I hear the background noise of slot machines and roulette wheels while walking through the casinos in Las Vegas, I think of college. Casinos and colleges have at least one thing in common—the odds are stacked in their favor and not just a little. They are stacked significantly against those of us with the money to play. Because of the odds, I want to arm you with the information you need to avoid the common mistakes in the admissions process that lead to families over paying.

> The number one mistake families make in the admissions application process is failing to appreciate the nature of the competition for being admitted to selective schools.

We have almost a million kids applying to fewer than one hundred schools, and some wonder why things don't work out the way they thought they would. Parents increase the likelihood of their student *not* being in the top 25 percent of the incoming freshman class when they apply to certain name-brand schools. We need to fish in ponds where the fish are, not where everyone is fishing.

A handful of colleges sit at the top of the pyramid and accept between 4 and 13 percent of students who apply for admission. The best you can hope for is that your number comes up once out of eight tries. Everyone who applies to these highly selective schools is brilliant, remarkable, a genius. It's like entering the HGTV Dream House sweepstakes—the odds are not in your favor. I'm not saying our kids shouldn't apply. I'm saying you're better off going into this knowing the probability of admission is low, and you will most likely pay retail if an acceptance letter does arrive. These schools don't need to discount the cost of attendance. The demand far exceeds their supply, and they can afford to be choosy.

Move down one tier of selectivity and the schools in this category are still only offering a seat to one out of every four applicants. This, however, is ripe territory for understanding how to play the game and adapt a more strategic approach. These schools are trying to break into the upper tier. Our brilliant, remarkable, genius student who is just like every other applicant for the most-sought-after schools will find themselves showered with offers of admission, as well as meaningful incentives, for applying to lesser-known brand names.

That leaves a third level of selectivity offering admission to one out of every two students who apply—still not a sure thing. This is where understanding the difference between in-state public schools and smaller, lesser-known private universities pays off. For many families, it's cheaper to attend a private college than default to a state university. It wasn't like this when we went to school, so we have no point of reference. But we need to understand the discounting that happens to put students in the classrooms and use it to our advantage.

Finally, we arrive at the least selective four-year institutions that admit 75 percent of those who apply. The student still must show they're interested in attending by doing a great job on the admissions application and meeting all the deadlines.

So, this high-stakes endeavor depends on a seventeen- or eighteen-year-old doing an excellent job on something they view as another paper for English class or the latest addition to their lengthy to-do list. Our students own this part of the project plan, but we can empower them with some tools for organizing their work, managing their deadlines and autographing their work with excellence.

2016-2017 Admissions Stats	2016	# Of	2015
College or University	Admit Rate	Applicants	Admit Rate
Stanford	4.70%	43,997	5.00%
Harvard	5.20%	39,041	5.30%
Columbia	6.00%	36,292	6.10%
Yale	6.30%	31,455	6.70%
Princeton	6.50%	29,303	7.10%
University of Chicago	7.60%	31,286	8.40%
MIT	7.80%	19,020	8.30%
Caltech	7.90%	6,856	8.80%
Brown	9.00%	32,380	9.50%
University of Pennsylvania	9.40%	38,918	10.20%
Pomona	9.20%	8,104	10.30%
Claremont McKenna	9.40%	6,342	11.00%
McMillan '18 — Duke	10.50%	32,105	11.80%
Dartmouth	10.50%	20,675	11.00%
Vanderbilt	10.50%	32,419	11.70%
Swarthmore	12.50%	7,717	12.50%
Northwestern	10.70%	35,099	13.20%
Johns Hopkins	11.50%	27,095	13.20%
Harvey Mudd	12.60%	4,180	13.00%
Pitzer	12.90%	4,142	13.50%
Amherst	13.80%	8,406	14.10%
Bates '17 Cornell	14.00%	44,966	15.10%
Bowdoin	14.30%	6,799	14.90%
Tufts	14.30%	20,223	16.10%
Washington University in St. Louis	15.20%	29,197	16.70%
University of California at Berkeley	15.80%	82,558	16.90%
Middlebury	16.00%	8,820	17.40%
Tarvus '18 Georgetown	16.40%	20,002	17.20%
Williams	17.30%	6,982	17.60%
University of Notre Dame	18.30%	19,499	19.80%
Cobo '17 Davidson	19.60%	5,614	22.10%
Carnegie Mellon	21.70%	21,189	23.70%
Carleton	22.60%	6,470	20.60%
Emory	24.70%	19,924	23.70%
Georgia Tech	25.30%	30,520	32.20%
Moser '18 American	25.70%	19,334	35.10%

SOURCE: Common Data Set, student newspapers, colleges and universities.
GRAPHIC: Nick Anderson - The Washington Post. Published April 5, 2016.

> ## The second biggest mistake families make is not managing expectations about the money.

Because most families don't take a strategic approach to developing the list of schools the student applies to, we find ourselves choosing before knowing the true cost involved. We don't handle any other six-figure financial decision in life this way. College is different because we don't think about it in a financial context. Our emotions tend to drive this decision.

Too often, a student applies and is accepted only to have the rug pulled out from under them when the financial aid award package arrives and the family realizes they cannot possibly make it work. Or worse, they don't realize the cash flow implications right away, the student starts school, and two years into it, reality hits home. Parents feel ashamed and embarrassed, the student is heartbroken, and younger siblings are told they can't go to certain schools because the money just isn't there. Deborah Caldwell wrote one of the best accounts of this scenario I've seen in a *Money* magazine blog.[7] Her experience hit the nail on the head.

Before your student completes an application for admission, you should know the probable out-of-pocket cost you are facing for the next four years. You should know whether you can even afford four years at that school. Why pay $75 for the privilege of carefully completing an application that will never result in accepting an offer of admission because of the cost?

---

7   Deborah Caldwell, "My Son Was Accepted to College He Can't Afford. Now What?" *Money*, May 3, 2016 (http://time.com/money/4315466/college-decision-day-son-accepted-afford/).

> # The third mistake families make is taking a deadline approach to preparing the admissions applications.

Too many students crank out admissions applications rather than craft them. Instead of allowing themselves the luxury of time and the opportunity to review, reconsider, and revise, they pray that the adrenaline rush of the deadline will be an ally in delivering a completed product. This is a place where your student can be competitive. If they take the time to prepare their materials thoughtfully, they will be better prepared than those who don't. Planning and executing are important skills to learn before spending six figures on their education.

There are several key elements of a well-crafted admissions application, including the essay or essays requested. In a system that relies heavily on quantitative data points (GPA, test scores, class rank), this is one qualitative area that allows the admissions committee to get to know your student as a person.

An essay for a college admissions application is *not* like the essays students write for English class. Their voice, personality, attitude, interests, and decision-making process must come through loud and clear for it to work in their favor. They have roughly ten paragraphs to share their unique identity and move the committee to put their application in the "Yes" pile. This is not a weekend project. It requires effort over time. Your student will benefit from guidance and coaching. This is one area where enlisting another set of eyeballs (or several) is a small investment that can yield a definite return.[8]

---

[8] If your student needs inspiration for writing the admissions essay, check out Top 42 Common App Admissions Essays - Study Notes, accessed February 15, 2017, https://www.apstudynotes.org/common-app/.

> # The fourth mistake families make is not understanding the concept of "demonstrated interest."

Demonstrated interest is a student's opportunity to show the college that he or she is sincerely interested in attending that school. Colleges that take this into account measure that interest through reliable, verifiable behaviors. They often use this measuring stick when considering tuition discounts and merit-based aid (more on these later in the book).

This criterion is foreign to most parents because this didn't exist when we went to school. Thanks to increased competition with the ability for students to apply through the Common Application, it's become an important, and often overlooked, element. While not universally used, it is becoming more important each year, and students can't afford to ignore it.

Introduced in 2007, the Common Application has steadily grown to be the standard route for students to apply to the six-hundred-plus member schools. If you want to apply to ten, twenty, or even fifty member schools, you can now do so with a single application. Students now apply to more schools because they can do so with one click of the mouse. Back in the day, people applied to three to five schools, tops; now, it's become a numbers game. The more schools you apply to, the more likely you are to get into one of them. This approach creates even more competition because everyone is applying everywhere. More isn't always better for the individual student or students overall.

The increased volume takes its toll on admissions committees. They used to review 7,000 applications for 2,500 seats, and now they are reviewing 21,000 applications for those same 2,500 seats. The admissions people need to filter through the applications more efficiently and say "no" a lot more often than ever before. The numbers are larger from a competition standpoint, too. What might have been considered an excellent essay out of a pool of 7,000 suddenly becomes mediocre in a sea of 21,000. A disproportionate number of applicants want to attend the same top-tier schools, which sets up a brand-name race to a broken bank account.

Demonstrated interest is a *verb*—it's what you do, not what you say. Here are a few key actions that demonstrate real interest to a college:

- Register on the school's website to receive information and marketing material.

- Attend a college fair and meet with college representatives.

- Write a follow-up email to the representatives the student met with.

- Fill out an information card at the college fair booth.

- Make an official campus visit (meaning one coordinated through the admissions office so the school has a record of the student's visit).

- When visiting, ask good questions and keep notes and calculate a score so that when the memory of that school begins to fade, you can recall the good, the bad, and the ugly.[9]

- Students should write a handwritten thank-you note to everyone they meet on the tour. (This may involve nagging, but it's worth it!)

- Apply early. "Early application" is recommended over "early decision." Early application demonstrates genuine interest; early decision is binding and eliminates negotiating options if an offer is made.

- Engage the admissions folks through social media platforms, which is an opportune time to clean up any student's online presence.

- Complete supplemental and optional essays when offered the opportunity to do so.

Imagine that you seek to hire a plumbing contractor for your kitchen remodel because you know he has the experience and know-how to handle a complicated job. You want to improve your chances of securing his services by proving you are serious and appreciate the value he brings. You would return his phone calls, sign the contract, and send the deposit with a personalized note. What measurable actions can your student take to send a clear signal that she wants to attend a specific school?

---

[9] Visit www.CenterforCollegeSolutions.com for a list of college visit questions and a scorecard.

> ## The fifth mistake families make is viewing college as a product instead of a project that creates the foundation for a future.

Even the language around college, "getting in," reveals the context from which we are driven. If we could make the subtle but important shift to a "getting from" mindset, our new operating principles would guide us to a more satisfying outcome. As my good friend and colleague Lisa Marker-Robbins, the founder of LEAP,[10] says, "Focus on the forty, not the four." The project called college has a definite beginning and end, but the whole reason we're doing it is to lay the foundation for the future.

Our students do not show up on campus and attend classes so an education can be bestowed upon them. The knowledge and critical-thinking skills must be earned, and it's theirs for the taking. However, that attitude and approach must be cultivated during the high school years. As parents, we can influence this aspect of the student's project plan.

To do so, we have to set aside the state high school graduation requirements. They represent the bare minimum necessary to "get out," not the opportunity to "get from." To be competitive, assume the student should take four years of history, four years of lab science (biology, physics, chemistry—not environmental, earth, or "other"), four years of math, four years of English, and

---

[10] Learning Enrichment & Assistance Program (LEAP), "About Us," retrieved October 22, 2016 (http://leapprogram.com/about.php). LEAP is a unique program where students of all ages who one day hope to pursue college can meet their academic needs and be supported outside the typical classroom setting.

four years of a foreign language. That's the lens the admissions committee is looking through.

If a student can get a *B+* or higher without struggling, they should probably be in an honors or Advanced Placement (AP) class. It doesn't make sense to take an abundance of honors or AP classes if the student's grades end up being all *B's*, though. Colleges still want to see *A's*. If the student is getting straight *A's* and the high school offers an International Baccalaureate (IB)[11] program, take advantage of the challenge and the real college preparation it can provide.

For most students, it's best to take higher-level courses in their areas of strength and regular courses for the rest. A good rule of thumb is to start with one or two honors courses in ninth grade. If they continue to demonstrate mastery and can handle the workload, add one higher-level course each year.

Don't get carried away with electives. Students should take classes in what interests them while staying focused on the core areas (history, lab sciences, math, English, and foreign language) because that's what colleges are looking for. High school is about laying the foundation for lifelong learning. It's about doing what it takes to "get from," not just what it takes to "get in."

---

[11] International Baccalaureate Organization (http://www.ibo.org/).

Key Steps to Prep for College Admission Success:

1. Understand the college selection process (the reality of the academic record, test results, affordability factors, merit-based opportunities, learning style).

2. Start early (college visits, high school course work, budgeted resources).

3. Have the context top of mind: why does the student want to go to college, and what do they want to accomplish?

   a. Fit: explore, experience, learning style, relative level of academic rigor, values the student for who they are

   b. Authenticity: what the student is sincerely interested in versus being driven by brand-name diploma

4. Manage expectations.

   a. Financial

   b. Acceptance

   c. Number of schools to apply to

5. Define "success" carefully and constructively.

   a. Self-worth is not defined by where a student goes or who accepts him or her.

   b. Love and support is not "conditional."

PROJECT PLAN ESSENTIALS

- We can avoid common mistakes and/or paying retail by being armed with the facts about preparing for college admissions.

- Our students own this part of the project.

- They will benefit from the wisdom, experience, and guidance of others.

- We can help them get organized, stay focused, and manage deadlines.

CHAPTER FOUR

GAIN SELF-
AWARENESS

A phone call from a client revealed the vital importance of self-awareness for students. Carol and Ken had been so excited to drive their son, Jacob, to college. Carol called me later and described how her son had sat in the back seat on the way home with tears streaming down his face.

Prior to the painful drive home, they had checked in with the resident assistant (RA) of Jacob's dorm, met his roommate, unpacked the car, and set up his side of the dorm room. Carol and Ken hugged Jacob good-bye and told him how much they loved him. Then, as they were about to drive off, misty eyed with the thought of their one and only son reaching this milestone, the dam broke.

Jacob had come unglued. He'd had a complete and utter meltdown.

He sobbed uncontrollably and begged his parents not to leave him. He refused to listen to any scenario that resulted in Mom and Dad leaving him at college while they drove home. After pleading and trying to reason with him, Ken and Carol felt they had no choice but to load the car back up with everything they had unpacked and head back to Las Vegas. They couldn't leave Jacob in Minnesota in this state of mind. They drove through the night, in silence, to return home. They simply didn't see it coming. Neither did I.

I was in my second year of helping parents figure out how they could pay for college. Ken, Carol, and I had developed a great cash flow strategy that allowed them to fund Jacob's four years at Carleton College. He wouldn't need to take out student loans because it was important to them that Jacob graduate debt free. They were still on track for Ken to retire at the age of sixty-five.

I was pretty proud of myself, actually. I felt like I had done a good job for them. I had done everything a financial adviser is trained to do.

But it wasn't enough.

We had neglected the most important piece of the college funding equation—the student. I didn't know Jacob had never spent a night away from home: no summer camp, no visiting relatives on his own, not even a sleepover at a friend's house.

I didn't know that the school had been his dad's idea. Or that Jacob didn't know what he wanted to study. Or that his mom was the one who helped him organize his week on Sunday nights. Those topics had never come up during our financial planning meetings. *Why would they?*

In my training for college funding, I learned about the importance of the expected family contribution and 529s and the use of financial aid and education tax credits. Anything having to do with the student was the domain of the school counselor or an independent education consultant. My licenses and regulatory rules of engagement kept me focused on the financial elements of the funding plan.

I didn't realize at the time how much the student drives the financial outcome of the funding plan. I was trying to solve an algebraic equation with only half the information and didn't even know it. Now—more than a decade later—I understand that we must integrate the needs of the student (academic and social fit of the college) with the resources of the parents to provide a real-world solution for the family. If we don't take both factors into consideration, even the best college-funding plan in the world will be derailed. The student could change majors several times, transfer from one school to another (with lost credits not accepted by the receiving university that must be repeated), require extra years of increasingly expensive school, or, worst of all, fail to graduate at all.

Imagine the parents' surprise when one of the first things I now recommend is to invest in an assessment process for the student. They've hired me to solve their financial challenges, so the assessment throws them for a loop. I'm not advocating a trivial personality profile survey, though. After lots of trial and error and field-tested results, I recommend a process used by the human resources departments of Fortune 500 companies to understand how to leverage their most valuable asset—human capital. The process has been adapted for high school students to identify probable majors for which they are best suited.

This philosophy is not new.

Our military administers an Armed Services Vocational Aptitude Battery (ASVAB) assessment to all new recruits. Before the Department of Defense accepts a recruit, it wants to know how the recruit will fit in the organization by assessing their strengths. Then it places the them in an area where they are most likely to succeed.

Perhaps we could ask the Department of Defense to talk to the Department of Education about the importance of assessments? Imagine scrapping the ACT and SATs and instead, require every high school junior to use this powerful science to lay the foundation for building their future.

I'll leave that to people skilled to fight those battles. What I can do is make you aware of the value of this tool so you can help your student.

Anything we can do to help our students increase their self-awareness is worthwhile. The same kinds of tests the military uses are critical for college and career planning. For research and out of interest, I have tried every behavioral assessment under the sun: Myers-Briggs Type Indicator, Kolbe, DISC, StrengthsFinder, Holland Codes, and even handwriting analysis. My go-to tool is the Birkman Method. It identifies how we are hardwired, where we're likely to thrive from a career perspective, and which majors support those career paths. I've had students as young as freshman and people well into their careers take the assessment.

Unless students understand who they are, what makes them tick, how to play to their strengths, and put themselves in an environment where they are likely to thrive, we are rolling the dice with our six-figure education investment.

We can't afford to leave this to chance.

Assessments are a terrific way to get started down the path of self-awareness and figuring out where an individual is heading. Most importantly, it helps to answer critical life questions such as "Why am I going to college?" and "What will I study when I get there?"

Our current education system and culture do not support cultivating self-awareness, so we have to foster this at home. As we do, our student's awareness of their thoughts, attitudes, emotions, beliefs, interests, and purpose grows. Then they will better understand their actions and behavior. This kind of knowledge develops over time and gradually shapes an individual's skills, interests, and values.

With certain exceptions, the laws of this country require young people to spend a minimum of twelve years honing knowledge and skills related to their intellectual intelligence (or IQ). That's the baseline. We need to help our students go beyond the minimal requirements to maximize the investment of time and money as it relates to higher education. We can't afford to pursue intellectual intelligence without making sure we include emotional intelligence (or EQ). Emotional intelligence includes the ability to identify emotions, both their own and other people's, and to use this knowledge for deciding what they think and do. Failing to focus on EQ misses the *big* picture. Decades of research now identifies EQ as the critical factor for success in both personal and professional life.

Failing to address the emotional and intellectual balance most often results in change of majors, transfers to another school, or dropping out of college. These outcomes are expensive: Changing majors can add time and money; transferring schools usually means lost credit, which is more time and money. And dropping out of school means money spent with little or no benefit and no marketable skills or employable degree.

Our institutions, both high school and higher education, focus almost exclusively on expanding knowledge associated with intellectual pursuits. In plain English, we legislate and outsource the development of our student's IQ-related skills. But what about their EQ?

No government programs or standards exist to support the development of those critical skills. This is one of those areas where we as parents can and should exert some influence. Today's students are distracted by a multitude of external forces: social media, celebrity culture, and their electronic leash (aka smartphone). We shouldn't underestimate the impact of what our kids are exposed to in the information age. It's not only higher education that is difficult to navigate, the entire world has changed since we sought a college degree.

Helping our kids develop clarity regarding their beliefs, motivations, and emotional responses to the world surrounding them saves us thousands of higher education dollars. Self-awareness means a student can look inside and identify what is unique about themselves. They recognize, appreciate, and manage their emotional "hardwiring." They adapt to new circumstances, and they know how to meet their needs, or advocate for themselves if necessary.

Coming to terms with who they are also involves accepting what they are not. Unfortunately, we don't do a good job—culturally or educationally—of holding up the mirror for young people. They need to face their personal reality, and we need to encourage them to work toward becoming the best version of themselves. The school systems do not champion this cause, so it's left to us as parents to facilitate this critical aspect of development.

HOW STUDENTS CAN DEVELOP SELF-AWARENESS:

1. Begin. Make it a priority.

Reading a book will not teach you how to know yourself. It's learned through doing and paying attention to your personal expressions of thought, emotions, and behavior. As parents, we need to accelerate that learning *before* we send our kids off to college. It's important because it's easier to make meaningful changes sooner, rather than later.

Most teenagers do not value solitude. Many of today's young people take their smartphones to bed with them, so the idea of being "unconnected" is not at all popular. Research regarding adolescents' experience confirms, however, that genuine "alone time" is an essential component of personal development and mental health. They aren't likely to volunteer for this exercise, but we can teach them a lot about creating boundaries and cultivating habits that will serve them well. We can have open discussions and model this behavior so they can see it in action. When they have to make those decisions for themselves, they'll be better off to have a foundation.

A great place to start is to expose your teenager to Johari window. (Ask them to search for the term on YouTube.[12] It'll get their wheels turning, and it's a medium they'll embrace.) The Johari Window is a communication model that is used to improve understanding between individuals. The word "Johari" is taken from the names of Joseph Luft and Harry Ingham, who developed the model in 1955.

There are two key ideas behind the tool:

1. You can build trust with others by disclosing information about yourself.

2. With the help of feedback from others, you can learn about yourself and come to terms with personal issues.

The Johari Window is shown as a four-quadrant grid, which you can see in the diagram on the following page.

---

12   The Start of Happiness, "Johari Window: A Self-Awareness Model," September 9, 2013 (https://www.youtube.com/watch?v=DEHh-vYGC20).

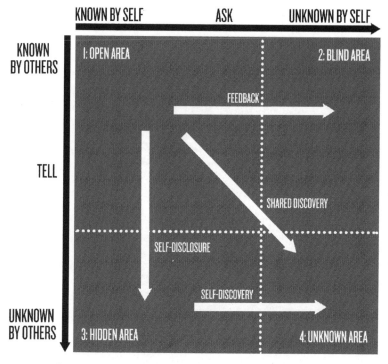

From "Of Human Interaction," by Joseph Luft. © 1969. Reproduced with permission from McGraw-Hill Education.

The four quadrants include the following:

I. Open Area (Quadrant I)

This quadrant represents the things you know about yourself and the things others know about you. This includes your behavior, knowledge, skills, attitudes, and "public" history.

2. Blind Area (Quadrant 2)

This quadrant represents things about you that you aren't aware of but that are known by others. This can include simple information or deep issues (for example, feelings of inadequacy, incompetence, unworthiness, or rejection), which are often difficult for individuals to face directly but can be seen by others.

3. Hidden Area (Quadrant 3)

This quadrant represents things you know about yourself, but others don't know.

4. Unknown Area (Quadrant 4)

This last quadrant represents things that are unknown to you and others.

The ultimate goal of the Johari Window is to enlarge the Open Area, without disclosing information that is too personal. That process is called "self-disclosure," and it's a give-and-take process between you and the people you interact with.

At first glance, the Johari Window may look like a complex tool, but it's easy to understand with a little effort and provides a visual reference people can use to look at their own character, and it illustrates the importance of sharing, being open, and accepting feedback from others. This is also a great way to open discussion with your teenager about how they relate to other people.

People who have a large Open Area are usually easy to talk to, they communicate honestly and openly with others, and they get along well with a group. People who have a very small Open Area are difficult to talk to, they seem closed off and uncommunicative, and they often don't work well with others because they're not trusted. Other people might have a large Blind Area with many issues that others can see clearly, but that haven't been identified or dealt with. They may have low self-esteem or anger issues when working with others.

2. Behave. Put it into practice.

Personal growth and testing self-sufficiency allows an individual to return to their community renewed, stronger, and wiser. Seemingly simple activities such as having teenagers fill out forms for high school, the doctor, or the dentist contribute to their sense of self-sufficiency. The same can be said for depositing money in their bank account and then asking them to manage and be responsible for payments related to car registration, car insurance, and school- or sports-related activities. Enrichment activities, like summer camp or a week-long program held on a college campus are beneficial because your teenager can test their independence in a safe environment. They learn about themselves when forced to interact with their peers in a new environment and step outside their comfort zone.

We tend to dismiss exercises like this as meaningless or not worth the hassle, but we underestimate the life lessons these simple tasks offer. Kids need to be allowed to navigate their day-to-day lives and assume more responsibility for themselves so they'll know how to function when they are out of the house and living on campus. They'll learn who they are as an adult and what their strengths and weaknesses are. I'll share more about this in chapter 12.

3. Believe. Talk about belief systems.

Self-awareness is a muscle that must be used frequently and consistently. Maya Angelou said, "When you know better, you do better." One of our greatest challenges is getting kids to understand that self-knowledge is their superpower, but this effort leads to the best possible outcome. Helping them craft a framework of personal values and beliefs provides a handsome return on investment. They'll be able to use that construct to navigate adulthood on training wheels (another term for college life). *This is the single most important element of the student part of the project plan.*

Here is an account of one parent's experience when her son struggled to decide what type of school would be best for him, his interests, and his skill set.

We began thinking seriously about our son's college arrangements at the end of his high school sophomore year. We focused most of our effort on getting our financial house in order. Our son had no idea what he wanted to study or where he wanted to attend. As parents, we recognized certain abilities that might reveal a career course. His strengths in math, science, critical thinking, and art seemed to point to architecture or engineering. Halfway through his junior year, he announced that he wanted to study film direction and/ or production. What? That seemed completely out of left field. He wasn't using free time to make short films or videos. He didn't show a particular interest in the science or business of the film industry. He didn't know anyone who had worked in the industry or studied the field.

Our son had just finished a semester exchange student program in western Africa, so maybe he was confused or unsettled about returning home. We couldn't figure it out but knew he needed to properly discern a study direction because engineering is a lot different than film.

After meeting with Beth Walker several times to work on precollege financial housekeeping, we remembered her describing Birkman/Fit2Flourish as a great resource to help narrow down career direction. Our son agreed to go through the process so we could better understand how he is hardwired and what careers might be a good match for his strengths.

The process was fantastic. It was comprehensive but not intimidating. It was interactive but not intrusive. It was systematized but still custom. The part our son dreaded the most was the career "homework," but once he got into it, he realized the Birkman/Fit2Flourish creators made it very doable even for a seventeen-year-old. They provided a great road map that guided his homework and clearly revealed a few strong career choices for him—one of which is film production!

The final Birkman report is a treasure trove of information about our son's inner workings. As parents, we were surprised to learn that the way our son processes information is to assume—usually incorrectly—that other people are on the same track as him. But we were relieved to learn that there are ways for us to be more specific with communication and actually get on the same track. We were not surprised to learn that our son has strong artistic aptitude, but we were pleasantly shocked to see that his artistic strength is best used in decision making and that this aptitude is so naturally strong that he absolutely must pursue a career that feeds his artistic side.

This Birkman report not only helped our son discern a strong career direction, but it also revealed the type of education environment that will give him the best chance to thrive. Our son prefers personal engagement, face-to-face communications, and opportunities to be part of a team. He is best suited for a small college campus where he can really get to know teachers and students. Our son prefers to have a starting point and an end goal along with clear rules and boundaries but wants flexibility in how he moves through the process. He is best suited for hands-on, experiential learning.

Beyond career discernment, we believe the personalized Birkman report has helped us be better parents; has helped him be a better son, brother, student, and employee; and ultimately will help him build stronger professional, peer, friend, and familial relationships throughout his life. To be able to see on paper his preferences and stresses related to a variety of components provides him a tremendous advantage in all aspects of his life.

—Gina S.

PROJECT PLAN ESSENTIALS

- Self-awareness reduces changing majors, transferring schools, and total time in college, which saves us money.

- Use assessment tools and enrichment experiences to help our kids become more self-aware.

CHAPTER FIVE

GET THE RIGHT MINDSET

 "She's worked so hard to get to this point," said Mrs. Matthews. "We want to support her in any way we can, but we don't want to see her make a huge mistake."

Marlene and Jerry Matthews came to see me because several colleges had offered their daughter, Allie, track scholarships. The athletic money offered was very similar, but the cost of the various schools was not. Their daughter had fallen in love with the most expensive school of the bunch.

"We've been very clear about how much money we have for college," Jerry said. "We are not willing to go into debt for her education, especially since she has more than one choice and can compete athletically at the collegiate level. We don't need to be put in the poor house. So, it would be her debt, not ours. She insists she's comfortable starting out in the hole, but I'm not sure she knows what that means."

I suggested I meet with Allie—without Mom and Dad.

It was easy to understand why multiple coaches were pursuing her. She was smart, attractive, quick to smile, and focused on her future. We talked at great length about the differences between the two schools that had made the best offers. Her favorite offered more name-brand recognition along with a much higher price tag. Even with the scholarship, it would be $20,000 *per year* over her parent's budget for college. Nevertheless, she was certain it was the place for her.

I knew her decision was not driven by logic. This determined young woman was not going to be persuaded with any argument I could muster. Mom and Dad sent her to me in hopes of a miracle, and I felt pretty useless. Allie was convinced that her times would improve, and the expensive college would offer more scholarship money during her sophomore and junior year.

I knew from experience how this might play out and said, "Promise me before you make your final decision, you'll call the coach at the big-name school and have a candid conversation with him about earning more scholarship money. Be sure to mention what the other school is offering. It might make a difference."

Several weeks after my meeting with Allie, Marlene sent a thank-you note and a gift card in the mail. She thanked me for suggesting Allie call the coach. Turns out, the coach was a stand-up guy. He told Allie she'd be crazy to pass up the other school's offer. It was unlikely she'd ever get more scholarship money from the big-name school, and incurring so much debt for her education simply wasn't a good idea. Marlene explained that Allie was disappointed by the conversation but accepted the wisdom of attending the other school. Marlene and Jerry were both relieved and thrilled with the outcome.

So what does any of this have to do with mindset?

Grit. Determination. The ability to bounce back from disappointment. The willingness to put yourself in a position to fail and learn from that experience.[13] Most seventeen-year-olds wouldn't have made that call to the coach because they wouldn't have wanted to risk hearing what he had to say.

Allie took responsibility and had an adult conversation, which resulted in an adult decision. She had to grapple with the question, "Do I do what I want to do because I want to do it? Or do I trust my mentors (my parents, coaches, other people with more life experience than me) who are suggesting an alternative idea that may serve me better in the long term?"

How many young people would've stayed on their preferred path, graduated with debt, and complained about the circumstances ten years down the road?

A few weeks before college started that fall, I received a second note with a familiar return address. This time it was from Allie. She said she was very thankful for my advice and was excited to be heading off to the other college. She couldn't wait to make the most of the opportunity.

---

13   Christine Carter, "Grit Needs Passion, Not Fear," Greater Good Science Center, University of California, Berkeley, August 30, 2016 (http://greatergood.berkeley.edu/article/item/grit_needs_passion_not_fear).

She possessed the mindset of a true champion.

Successful athletes understand the sacrifices, the setbacks, and the need to pick themselves up, dust themselves off, and try again. Not all students are athletes, but all students can adopt a winning mindset. Dr. Christine Carter, the author of *The Sweet Spot: How to Find Your Groove at Home and Work*, says, "Passionless persistence might lead to achievement, but will it make you happy?"

Jacob, the student who rode back to Nevada with his parents before the first day of college, didn't know what he was capable of. His lack of self-awareness and confidence was debilitating. He hadn't developed or tested his mindset muscle to allow him to perform in a new environment. But here's the thing: Jacob can learn to react to situations in life just like Allie did. His meltdown in Minnesota kicked off a different kind of education. As uncomfortable as the situation was, as embarrassed as he may have felt, his self-awareness grew exponentially from that experience because he activated his mindset muscle in a meaningful way.

We have to help our kids think beyond merely "getting in" and focus on the forty years that will follow college, not the four. Instead, get them in the mindset of sucking their college experience dry of every benefit it can possibly provide. Imagine a world where kids set foot on campus with a sense of purpose and a plan to wring out every last drop of value they possibly can—where "getting from" is the way they roll.

Mindset is how kids program their behavior and manage their emotions. It's a proactive, intentional effort toward achieving what they want (which, of course, depends on self-awareness). A student gathers information from a variety of sources and decides on a course of action for themselves; a follower lives in accordance with someone else's predetermined plan.

The students have to do the work, and we have to hold them accountable for doing it. When we do, they won't drop out, give in to peer pressure, or take six years to get a four-year degree. And we'll save a small fortune.

Wedding Syndrome by Seth Godin

Running a business is a lot more important than starting one.

Choosing and preparing for the job you'll do for the next career is a much more important task than getting that job. Serving is more important than the campaign.

And a marriage is always more important than a wedding.

It's tempting to focus on the product launch, on the interview, on the next thing—tempting but ultimately a waste.

Our culture is organized around transitions, but they're a distraction. What it says on your wedding invitation doesn't matter a whole lot in the long run.

Google the word *mindset* and you'll find the work of Dr. Carol Dweck, a leading expert and author on the topic.[14] She is one of many resources at our disposal to support the development of a healthy mindset. Adults hire life coaches because they understand the value of having someone guide them through a process of

---

14 Carol Dweck, "Mindset," retrieved October 22, 2016 (http://mindsetonline.com/).

self-discovery and self-actualization. Our children should have the same navigational tools.

If we are about to make a six-figure investment in education, doesn't it make sense to set aside both time and money to get the best return? I've learned that it makes a difference. A small investment in mindset during the high school years saves tens of thousands of dollars during the college years.

Key Tools for Mindset Development:

1. Intention: Set out with the end in mind, rather than just showing up and letting things happen.

2. Push personal boundaries: Get comfortable being uncomfortable.

3. Surround yourself with smart people: Cultivate and consult an informal board of advisers whose only objective is guiding you to your best possible outcome.

4. Hold the vision: Visualize a bigger, brighter future for yourself.

5. Follow through: Turn thoughts into action.

6. Commit to always learning: Realize there are two educations—the one you get from school and the one you craft for yourself.

PROJECT PLAN ESSENTIALS

- Getting into college is not the goal.

- Getting a great education that catapults our child into a productive, satisfying future is the opportunity college provides.

- Cultivating this mindset is something we can invest in during the high school years.

PART II:

THE PARENTS

Estimate Family Contribution

Apply for Financial Aid

Assess Retirement Readiness

Calculate Cash Flow for College

You cannot teach a man anything; you can only help him find it within himself.

—GALILEO GALILEI

It's appropriate that the origin of the word *coach* is rooted in the Hungarian village of Kocs, where an unknown carriage maker designed a larger, more comfortable carriage. Parents are their children's ultimate coach, something, or someone, who carries a valued person from where they are to where they want to be. We are literally and figuratively carrying our kids to their future.

A Coach by any other name . . .

Japan	sensei	=	one who has gone further down the path
Sanskrit	guru	=	one with great knowledge and wisdom
Tibet	lama	=	one with spirituality and authority to teach
Italy	maestro	=	master teacher of music
Greece	mentor	=	a wise and trusted adviser

Every culture reveres the coaching role that we are asked to play as parents. The challenge is not new and seems even more important in the "urgent vs. important" culture we live in. To comfortably carry our precious cargo from the land of adolescence to the world of adulthood, we find ourselves crossing the bridge called college. Our modern-day spring suspensions, designed to deliver a smooth ride and ensure delivery at the desired destination, are largely financial. We find ourselves challenged to forge and shape a carriage of a different sort—one that allows us to maintain our current lifestyle, continue funding our future retirement, and take on the increasingly ambitious task of paying for college.

The critical components parents need to focus on are knowing their Expected Family Contribution (EFC), answering the four critical questions regarding retirement, developing a cash flow plan for college, and understanding how and why every family should apply for financial aid.

CHAPTER SIX

ESTIMATE FAMILY CONTRIBUTION

Imagine that the Jones family needs to replace their kitchen floor after an unfortunate dishwasher incident. Looking to make lemonade out of the lemons, they decide to combine the insurance settlement with some money they have in savings to remodel the entire kitchen. They envision a kitchen that is more efficient, has all the latest amenities, and looks appropriate for the neighborhood.

While perusing design magazines, Mr. Jones spots a matching set of premium appliances he thinks he can't do without. He also finds great reviews on his favorite on-line review sites. His co-worker, Mr. Smith mentioned that the higher-end appliances are great for resale value, so Mr. Jones moves them from the nice-to-have column to the must-have column.

With visions of a stainless steel range with matching dual ovens in his near future, Mr. Jones finds a contractor who sells and installs the appliances in this particular line. Great news! He signs on the dotted line to have them delivered and installed.

Eight weeks later, with construction dust everywhere and dirty dishes in the bathtub, Mr. Jones begins to understand that the insurance reimbursement wasn't what he expected and the new winter tires for his wife's car took a bite out of the savings account that had been earmarked for the remodel. He realizes that the cabinets, countertops, fixtures and flooring that looked so good with his new appliances far exceeded their "budget" and he needs to resort to credit cards to finish the project.

What Mr. Jones doesn't fully appreciate is the opportunity cost of the total kitchen remodel. Those extra debt payments today will likely mean Mr. and Mrs. Jones will have to delay retirement for at least two years. The expensive gas range won't provide them with interest and dividends that can be used to supplement social security when they turn 67. Their current lifestyle expenses are robbing their future lifestyle funding; he's paying compound interest instead of earning it.

Now imagine the project wasn't a kitchen remodel but college. Mr. Jones would have kicked things off with his Expected Family Contribution (EFC)[15] instead of the money from the

---

15   EDspertise, LLC, "EFC Calculator," retrieved October 22, 2016 (https://www.aidcalc.com/EFC.aspx).

insurance company. The EFC is your starting point because it's the minimum out-of-pocket cost the colleges believe you should pay every year. Knowing your EFC helps you formulate a game plan for getting from where you are to where you want to be. The EFC is a number calculated by the Department of Education or the College Board based on the information they collect on the financial aid forms.

Many parents fail to calculate the EFC and head blindly toward the admissions process. They spend their time and money and find out later they should have been looking at a different range of schools because of what they will be expected to pay. They feel disheartened by what they should've done. There are better ways to approach this, methods that can deliver a much easier, more satisfying experience. Understanding this can help you avoid these mistakes.

Turns out, the Department of Education and most American families are on opposite ends of the spectrum for calculating what is "affordable" where college is concerned. Unfamiliar to most parents, the EFC is the *minimum amount* a student is expected to contribute toward the cost of college. It is based on both the parents' and the student's income and assets, the size of the family, and number of students currently attending college in your household. You must calculate and report this data every year the student(s) attend school to be eligible for any financial aid (I'll cover applying for financial aid in chapter 7). Circumstances change—people get divorced, laid off, a sibling also starts college—so it's like nailing jelly to the wall. This critical element of your overall funding plan can be a bit of an enigma. Nonetheless, we need to understand what it is and the role it will play in our efforts.

Familiarize yourself with the following critical college math equation:

COA	**Cost of Attendance** (tuition, fees, room and board, miscellaneous fees)
– EFC	**Expected Family Contribution** (calculation based on data provided)
Need	Gap, if any, between the cost and what is expected from the family

---

This seemingly simple equation can get confusing because you might need to use three different formulas for the EFC depending on which college your student applies to. The minimum out-of-pocket cost for college, or EFC, is a *range,* not a single number, because different schools calculate it differently (more on this in chapter 7). The range you land in will determine your planning priorities based on the categories for need-based financial aid: ALWAYS, SOMETIMES, or NEVER.

2017-2018 FEDERAL EFC QUICK REFERENCE TABLE

NUMBER OF DEPENDENT CHILDREN

AGI	1	2	3	4	
$30,000	$998	$0	$0	$0	
$32,500	$1,435	$582	$0	$0	
$35,000	$1,871	$1,018	$0	$0	
$37,500	$2,307	$1,455	$666	$0	
$40,000	$2,733	$1,891	$1,103	$0	
$42,500	$3,142	$2,328	$1,539	$625	
$45,000	$3,074	$2,739	$1,975	$1,061	
$47,500	$3,539	$3,148	$2,399	$1,498	
$50,000	$4,004	$3,081	$2,808	$1,934	
$52,500	$4,412	$3,545	$3,217	$2,343	
$55,000	$4,951	$4,010	$3,624	$2,752	
$57,500	$5,383	$4,419	$3,972	$3,161	NEED-BASED AID ELIGIBILITY AT
$60,000	$6,015	$4,958	$4,511	$3,096	2 YR PUBLIC, 4 YR PUBLIC, 4 YR PRIVATE, ELITE 4 YR COLLEGES
$62,500	$6,500	$5,391	$5,050	$3,560	
$65,000	$7,244	$6,023	$5,499	$4,025	
$67,500	$7,834	$6,510	$6,131	$4,437	
$70,000	$8,708	$7,253	$6,636	$4,976	
$72,500	$9,581	$7,846	$6,636	$5,412	
$75,000	$10,455	$8,719	$7,380	$6,044	
$80,000	$12,202	$10,466	$8,867	$7,277	
$85,000	$13,949	$12,214	$10,615	$8,747	
$90,000	$15,697	$13,961	$12,362	$10,495	
$95,000	$17,219	$15,655	$14,109	$12,242	
$100,000	$18,731	$17,168	$15,740	$13,989	
$105,000	$20,244	$18,680	$17,252	$15,557	
$110,000	$21,756	$20,192	$18,764	$17,069	
$115,000	$23,268	$21,587	$20,159	$18,464	
$120,000	$24,016	$22,218	$20,790	$19,095	

2017-2018 FEDERAL EFC QUICK REFERENCE TABLE

NUMBER OF DEPENDENT CHILDREN

AGI	1	2	3	4	
$125,000	$25,677	$24,165	$22,330	$20,635	NEED-BASED AID ELIGIBILITY AT
$130,000	$27,335	$25,301	$23,874	$22,175	2 YR PUBLIC, 4 YR PUBLIC,
$135,000	$28,993	$26,959	$25,414	$23,719	4 YR PRIVATE, ELITE 4 YR COLLEGES
$140,000	$30,651	$28,617	$26,954	$25,259	
$145,000	$32,309	$30,275	$28,495	$26,800	NEED-BASED AID ELIGIBILITY AT
$150,000	$33,967	$31,933	$30,035	$28,340	4 YR PUBLIC, 4 YR PRIVATE
$155,500	$35,578	$33,544	$31,646	$29,833	AND ELITE 4 YR COLLEGES
$160,000	$37,180	$35,155	$33,257	$31,327	
$165,000	$38,721	$36,738	$34,868	$32,760	
$170,000	$40,261	$38,279	$36,432	$34,077	
$175,000	$41,802	$39,819	$37,973	$35,512	
$180,000	$43,342	$41,359	$39,513	$36,947	
$185,000	$44,882	$42,900	$40,976	$38,381	
$190,000	$46,423	$44,440	$42,410	$39,816	NEED-BASED AID ELIGIBILITY AT
$195,000	$48,010	$46,028	$43,892	$41,298	4 YR PRIVATE AND ELITE 4 YR COLLEGES
$200,000	$49,598	$47,615	$45,374	$42,779	
$205,000	$51,185	$49,182	$46,855	$44,261	
$210,000	$52,772	$50,664	$48,337	$45,743	
$215,000	$54,360	$52,145	$49,819	$47,224	
$220,000	$55,947	$53,627	$51,300	$48,706	
$225,000	$57,535	$55,109	$52,782	$50,188	
$230,000	$59,015	$56,552	$54,226	$51,631	
$235,000	$60,438	$57,975	$55,649	$53,054	
$240,000	$61,861	$59,398	$57,072	$54,477	
$245,000	$63,284	$60,821	$58,494	$55,900	
$250,000	$64,707	$62,244	$59,917	$57,323	
$275,000	$71,821	$69,359	$67,032	$64,438	NEED-BASED AID ELIGIBILITY AT ELITE 4 YR COLLEGES

NO NEED-BASED AID ELIGIBILITY

If you fall into the LIGHTEST GRAY range, you are most likely an ALWAYS household, meaning you will always qualify for NEED-BASED financial aid. Your planning priorities are to minimize your EFC, optimize your aid eligibility, and make sure you file your financial aid forms long before the school and government deadlines (which may differ).

If you fall into the LIGHT GRAY or GRAY ranges, you are a SOMETIMES household, meaning sometimes you'll qualify for NEED-BASED financial aid, and sometimes you won't. Your planning priorities are applying to schools with a history of offering merit-based aid or tuition discounts to students like yours, making sure your student takes only four years to earn a four-year degree, and being as efficient with cash flow as possible during the college years.

If you fall into the DARK GRAY or DARKEST GRAY range, you are a NEVER household, meaning you will never qualify for NEED-BASED financial aid. Your planning priorities include creating tax scholarships through income- and asset-shifting strategies, applying to colleges with a history of offering financial incentives or tuition discounts to students like yours, and making sure your student takes only four years to earn their four-year degree.

Unfortunately, most families make the mistake of applying to schools before they've calculated their EFC, like when Mr. Jones outfitted his kitchen with premium appliances before confirming all the related costs. Imagine bidding for some rare, sought-after artwork at a Sotheby's auction without knowing the price to which you're committing. Shock and awe morphs into disbelief, disappointment, debt, and finally, a sense of defeat. It doesn't have to be this way. Even though the process is confusing, it is worth your while to understand the EFC range for your household so you can avoid paying retail for college.

The purpose of this chapter is to prevent the EFC from coming as a surprise. Parents should calculate their EFC early and often. I recommend calculating it in January of your oldest child's sophomore year of high school at the latest, but you can calculate it any time before then for planning. You can find a variety of EFC calculators available online, but I suggest using the College Board's[16] because it will generate both the federal and the institutional answers for you.

Don't be lulled into thinking the EFC will be your out-of-pocket cost for college. Most schools won't help you address the gap between what college actually will cost and your EFC. To arrive at your most likely scenario, add another 25 to 50 percent to the EFC figure. Then inflate that number 5 percent for each year there are kids attending college.

Let me give you an example: Stonehill College is a private Catholic college in Easton, Massachusetts that boasts a 94 percent employment rate one year after graduation for students who sought employment and an 89 percent acceptance rate for graduates who applied to graduate schools.[17] The annual cost of admission, or retail price, is $55,670. Assume your family has calculated an EFC of $6,202. This is the bare minimum you would pay for your student to attend. Your need, that is the gap between the cost of admission and your EFC is $49,468. Your probable out-of-pocket expenses will be closer to $25,270 (with loans) to $30,770 (without loans). Even for a more economical school, like Framingham State University with an annual cost of

---

16   The College Board, "EFC Calculator," retrieved October 22, 2016 (https://bigfuture.collegeboard.org/pay-for-college/paying-your-share/expected-family-contribution-calculator).

17   2015 figures found on the college's website, retrieved February 17, 2017 (http://www.stonehill.edu).

$22,924, and an EFC of $5,245, most likely you will still pay $10,124 to $16,824 in out-of-pocket expenses.

Is this a perfect system? No. The engineers among us will shudder at the lack of detail and simplistic approach. But it's a helpful context to develop a cash flow plan for college. For most families, about 98 percent in fact, could use this estimated number.

Knowing your EFC is square one for creating a college-funding plan. It's the foundation for making decisions related to fit—academically, socially, and financially. Once you know which category you fall into—ALWAYS. SOMETIMES, or NEVER - your planning priorities for financing higher education will become clear. The strategies are identified in this table and discussed in case studies below.

Planning Priorities

	Optimize Aid Eligibility	School Selection	Tax Scholarships	Cash Flow Efficiency
Category 1 Always	1	2		3
Category 2 Sometimes	3	1		2
Category 3 Never		2	1	3

Case Study #1: Planning for an ALWAYS Household

Paul is the proud father of three kids, and he and his wife, Janice, live well within their means. Paul recently assumed responsibility for his father's business and enlisted Janice's help to run the day-to-day operations. They take home about $80,000 a year but have managed to save some money for retirement, and they have almost $90,000 in Uniform Transfer to Minors Act (UTMA) accounts for their kids. Paul firmly believes that "college isn't optional in my household."

When we met, Paul and Janice had three financial goals in mind:

1. Get the kids through college with little or no student loan debt.

2. Make significant and consistent contributions to their retirement accounts.

3. Pay down their mortgage.

Little did they know saving money for their kids in UTMA accounts actually drove their EFC higher and limited their financial aid eligibility. That is, being responsible and saving for their children's education counts against them when it comes to need-based funding. Because UTMA accounts are considered the student's assets (kids assume control of UTMA accounts at age eighteen in most states), the financial aid formulas assess those assets more heavily. The financial aid formulas assume that if students have money in their name, those funds most certainly will be used for college. The result is that the family is penalized because they saved money.

They moved the money to accounts that are not considered in the financial aid formula.[18] Swift action reduced the family's expected contribution (EFC) between 18 percent to 48 percent (depending on the school's individual formula), and increased their aid eligibility by $130,000 over the nine years their kids would be in college. The money was still accessible. It kept earning interest, was still earmarked for college, and offered a death benefit in the unlikely event that Janice passed away before the kids finished college—all positive outcomes for the kids.

We simply made it "vanish" from the family balance sheet for reporting purposes on the Free Application for Federal Student Aid (FAFSA) and the College Scholarship Service (CSS) Profile (more about those forms later). Now they can direct cash flow that would've gone toward college debt, most likely in the form of Parent PLUS loans, and direct it toward retirement.

> **The priorities for a family in ALWAYS category are as follows:**

1. **Keep the EFC as low as possible**. Many times, that means shifting nonretirement assets or home equity to increase aid eligibility. It's rare to put effort or energy into decreasing income; in those circumstances where income is noticeably lower (because of divorce, job loss, disability, etc.), we can make lemonade (eligibility for more financial aid) out of those lemons (lower income).

---

[18] In this case, a permanent life insurance contract called a modified endowment contract. Please note that life insurance and annuities are notoriously "oversold" as a solution for reducing a family's EFC; individual facts and circumstances must be considered before any given strategy is implemented.

2. **School selection** remains important because most schools do *not* meet 100 percent of the unmet need through the need-based financial aid system, so any merit-based aid can help close any remaining funding gap. Chapter 9 will go into much greater detail on this matter.

Case Study #2: Planning for a SOMETIMES Household

Jeff makes just over $100,000 as the sales manager for a midsize technology company. Lydia brings home $45,000 as a science teacher. They have two children. Jason is a junior in high school, and Katie is an eighth grader. Over the last four years, they've let their credit card debt amass to more than $20,000. However, a rebounded real estate market and twelve years of mortgage payments gave them some nice home equity on their balance sheet. They both contribute to their retirement accounts through work, and Jeff has an IRA from a 401(k) rollover from a previous employer.

Now that Jason is a junior, college has come into focus for their household, and they are beginning to think about the realities of sending him to school.

"If we had $2,000 a month to put toward college, we wouldn't be talking to you!" That was Lydia's comment when I calculated their EFC. Like so many families I work with, the minimum out-of-pocket cost assigned to them through the financial aid formulas far exceeded their expectations in terms of price tag. Showing parents their EFC for the first time is like ripping off a Band-Aid. It stings at first, but eventually, it stops hurting.

Jeff and Lydia have reason to be optimistic.

Jason is a good student and tests well. He's taking a few honors courses and one advanced placement class. If he maintains his grade point average, scores well on the ACT and/or SAT tests, and applies to schools with a history of giving students like him lots of free money (financial aid that doesn't need to be paid back), he's likely to be offered meaningful scholarship money.

Jeff and Lydia can become much more efficient with their money while also lowering their EFC at the private universities Jason is interested in. Some of their options include refinancing their house, pulling out enough of the equity to pay off nondeductible, high-interest debt to free up almost enough cash flow to meet their EFC (money that was going toward the credit card debt every month). They can secure a home equity line of credit (HELOC) that provides cash flow in the event of an emergency or covers rising costs as the younger kids enter college. That debt is low interest and tax deductible with interest-only payments. It will allow them to pay the debt down on their schedule, not the federal government's.

Most importantly, they can maintain their current lifestyle, continue to make contributions toward their retirement, and make college an affordable reality for both Jason and Katie. They had the right pieces of the puzzle; they just needed a little help putting it together.

Most of the families I work with fall into the SOMETIMES category. They make a good living but not so good that paying for college isn't a challenge. Jeff and Lydia are a perfect example.

The priorities of any family in this category are as follows:

1. **School selection.** Applying to colleges and universities likely to offer our kids merit-based aid (free money in

the form of grants, scholarships, and tuition discounts) is critical for SOMETIMES households. Combine that with schools where students are likely to get a four-year degree in four years, and we've got a good thing going. Graduation rates matter, and we need to pay attention to them because an extra year or two of college is expensive. (Again, because this is such an important topic, I've devoted chapter 9 to strategically selecting colleges for application.)

2. **Cash flow efficiency.** Most of us are losing money unknowingly and unnecessarily. Once identified, it can be brought back to help pay for college.

3. **Keep the EFC as low as possible.** Strategic repositioning of assets and home equity can result in more financial aid. For families with more than one child to put through college, this can be substantial and should not be ignored.

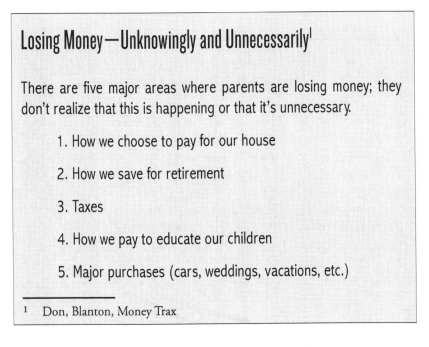

Losing Money—Unknowingly and Unnecessarily[1]

There are five major areas where parents are losing money; they don't realize that this is happening or that it's unnecessary.

1. How we choose to pay for our house

2. How we save for retirement

3. Taxes

4. How we pay to educate our children

5. Major purchases (cars, weddings, vacations, etc.)

[1]   Don, Blanton, Money Trax

Conventional wisdom and cultural practice perpetuate these wealth transfers. What I mean is that we transfer our hard-earned money away from us and to institutions: mortgage companies, banks, credit card companies, lenders like GMAC and Toyota Credit, and, of course, colleges.

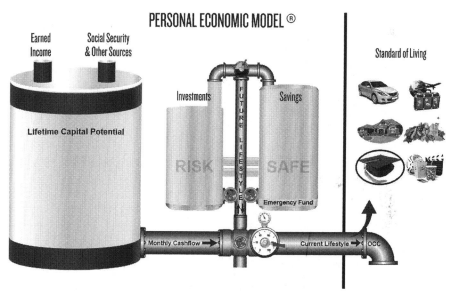

Personal Economic Model® is the property of MONEYTRAX. Permission granted to licensed users only; details available at MoneyTrax.com

What most parents fail to comprehend is that we are crossing the line. We interrupt the compounding we need to fund our future lifestyle by transferring money from our savings and investment tanks for lifestyle choices. Every time we do that, we give our money to the institutions and allow them to use our money for their benefit, not ours.

Human beings are creatures of convention, and conventional thinking often puts us in the poor house, hence the terms unknowingly and unnecessarily. If we understood how money works in our lives, we wouldn't keep doing this! A subtle paradigm shift that involves using money earmarked for lifestyle to pay for lifestyle expenses can solve the challenge most parents face when it comes to paying for college.

Too often, we shrug our shoulders, accepting what we perceive to be our only choices. Well-meaning parents reluctantly agree to the terms of the Parent Plus Loan being offered by colleges (perhaps the only area where the federal government makes a profit) or resign ourselves to the fact that we'll have to work another ten years past our target retirement date.

Three or four years before your child goes to college is the ideal time to bring the five areas of wealth transfer into laser focus and find money that can rightfully be brought back to your household so you can support the cash flow trifecta: retirement, college and current lifestyle.

In that order.

Solving this cash flow riddle is perhaps the most important thing parents can do as college hurtles down the track towards our front door. This kind of clarity is the result of a detailed analysis of what's coming in, where it's going, and why. Once we understand those three things, the how can be configured correctly. As creatures of habit, we often don't see or hear the drip, drip, drip of the leaks in our financial life, so an objective third party is often needed to provide perspective on the situation and challenge the assumptions that allowed this to happen in the first place.

Said another way, figuring out how to pay for college is a gift, though most parents don't see it that way. Because it's wrapped in complexity, stress, and the emotion that comes with having a teenager managing a significant portion of the project, we often overlook the opportunity it presents. This is the perfect time to get our financial house in order and make the mid-course corrections that are inevitably necessary.

Lifestyle money for lifestyle expenses. Don't cross the line.

Case Study #3: Planning for a NEVER Household

If you are a successful business owner, doctor, lawyer, dentist, or highly compensated executive, you probably fall into the NEVER category. Once the adjusted gross income for a household exceeds $250,000, Uncle Sam's help all but evaporates.

Like Bill Gates or any other billionaire, if you fill out the forms, your student will be eligible for unsubsidized student loans. This can help your child establish credit, have some "skin in the game," and give you access to low-interest cash flow for college.

Ideally, you will look to the tax code to create cash flow during the college years. By shifting income or assets (or both) to your child, you can create a tax scholarship, meaning you redirect funds that were leaving your bank account in the form of an IRS tax payment and reroute those funds to the college of choice.

These strategies require real tax planning, not just competent tax reporting. As we approach the college years, we need to be proactive about tax liabilities rather than calculate them based on what we see in the rearview mirror.

Dr. Jerry Evans is an orthodontist who is married to Lucy, a successful real estate agent. They have three beautiful kids: Benjamin is seventeen, Charlotte is fourteen, and Eva is twelve. Their combined income is around $350,000 a year, making their EFC higher than the cost of attendance at all the schools the kids are likely to attend.

We looked at several strategies to shift income and assets to the kids before and during college to create tax scholarships. The tax code allows students to file independently (within a lower tax bracket) if they can show "half of their support," meaning that they provide at least half their expenses during the year.

That's important for the reasons below:

1. "Half of their support" is easy to calculate during the college years because each school publishes a cost-of-attendance figure that you can split in half. If the cost-of-attendance for Creighton University is $48,722, for example, a student would have to make a little more than $24,000 per year to file his or her own tax return.

2. The kid's tax bracket is substantially lower than that of their parents, so the family can gain real tax savings on the same money coming into the household that they can reroute toward college expenses. Four to six thousand dollars per year times three kids for four years of college starts to add up.

3. The student is eligible for education tax credits that are phased out for the parents after $180,000 in adjusted gross income. At $2,500 per year, that's an additional $10,000 over the four years of college that the family realizes from shifting income into the child's lower tax bracket.

Most parents follow the logic up to this point but often ask me, "What can my son or daughter do for me to justify paying them $24,000 a year, especially if they are in school nine to ten months of the year?" This is where the family's tax adviser is critical. Everything must be done correctly: paying all the appropriate taxes, documenting the job responsibilities, and doing things by the book. We want to use the rules for our cash flow advantage, not skirt them.

For the Evans family, we looked at gifting equipment from the dental practice to an LLC that the kids owned and renting it back to Dr. Evans. That strategy proved too complicated and their certified public accountant (CPA) nixed it. The parents also owned several income-producing rental properties that could be used. They formed an LLC to hold the rental real estate and made the kids members of the entity. Jerry and Lucy were the managing members but didn't receive much of the income. The rental income went primarily to the kids, bypassing Mom and Dad's higher income tax bracket. They reported the income in the lower bracket for the kids. The CPA loved the idea, comfortable with paying the kids through the rental income.[19]

The Evans family will redirect more than $100,000 toward college that would've otherwise gone to the Internal Revenue Service. Now that's a tax scholarship!

---

[19] Tax scholarship strategies necessarily involve the family's tax adviser.

> ## The priorities of any family in the NEVER category are as follows:

1. **Tax scholarships.** When the EFC exceeds the cost of attendance at any school, it's time to disregard the financial aid formulas and focus on strategic income and asset shifting.

2. **School selection.** Please see chapter 9 for an in-depth plan.

3. **Cash flow efficiency.** Find the money you are losing unknowingly and unnecessarily and redirect it toward college and retirement.

*Refer to the Success Plan Timeline on page 86 and 87.

PROJECT PLAN ESSENTIALS

- Knowing your minimum out-of-pocket cost is your starting point.

- Your planning priorities will be dictated by the category of aid in which you find yourself.

CENTER FOR
COLLEGE
SOLUTIONS

Refer to Guidance Notes for details	SOPHOMORE YEAR											
	AUG	SEP	OCT	NOV	DEC	JAN	FEB	MAR	APR	MAY	JUN	JUL
						BASE YEAR FOR FINANCIAL						
Calculate EFC	■	■	■	■	■							
Assess Retirement Readiness	■	■	■	■	■							
Calculate College Cash Flow	■	■	■	■	■							
Calendar Issues: Vacations, Visits, Etc.												
College Major & Career Assessments												
Prep & Take PSAT/NMSQT												
Review Curriculum Strength for Grades 11 & 12												
Review PSAT/NMSQT Results												
Student Competitive Position (CAP Index)												
Establish Test Strategy: ACT vs. SAT												
Identify College Search Criteria												
Start Initial College Search												
Prepare for SAT/ACT												
Take SAT/ACT												
College Research & Evaluation												
Letters of Recommendation Requested												
Spring College Visits												
Summer College Visits												
Finalize College List												
Register for Common Application												
ID Admissions & Financial Aid Deadlines												
Fall College Visits												
College Interviews - Fall Senior Year												
Draft Common Application Personal Essay												
Identify & Begin Writing Additional Essays												
Advisor Reviews Common Application												
Submit Common Application												
Register For CSS Profile												
Complete CSS Profile												
Registration: FSA ID for FAFSA												
Complete & Submit FAFSA												
Evaluate Financial Aid Awards												
Make Final College Visits if Necessary												
Final Decision & Enrollment Deposit												
Decide on First Year Financing Options												

SUCCESS PLAN TIMELINE
for College Bound Students

	JUNIOR YEAR												SENIOR YEAR								
AUG	SEP	OCT	NOV	DEC	JAN	FEB	MAR	APR	MAY	JUN	JUL	AUG	SEP	OCT	NOV	DEC	JAN	FEB	MAR	APR	MAY

ID ELIGIBILITY

If Required

Planning for Success: *This project plan provides you with the ideal time to complete each milestone and who is responsible for each activity.*

- Student Responsibility
- Family Responsibility
- Parent Responsibility

www.centerforcollegesolutions.com

CHAPTER SEVEN

APPLY FOR
FINANCIAL AID

I f you're sending kids to college, you should apply for financial
aid. Every year you have kids in school, regardless of which
category of need-based aid you fall into, you need to file. Your
strategy and reasons for applying may differ from your neighbor's,
but filing is not an option.

Admittedly, it's like volunteering for a root canal—no one
would blame you for wanting to avoid the labyrinth that the

application process has become. The current state of financial aid in the US university system is the poster child for unintended consequences, and despite the best of intentions to make college an affordable reality for students from a broad range of families, the process is far from user-friendly. As parents of college-bound students, we need to understand how the process works and what we need to do to make the most of what's available to us. Before I show you how to do that, it helps to understand how we got here.

The story behind financial aid is longer than you might think, but the important thing to understand is that the federal government's involvement in financing higher education is relatively new from a historical perspective. Before the end of World War II, the US supported higher education through land grants in the nineteenth century to found or support state schools, offering programs in agriculture, engineering, and military tactics. Private scholarship endowments and school-sponsored loan systems had been the norm to provide direct funding for students who otherwise couldn't have attended.

The government's role changed drastically when Congress enacted the GI Bill, officially known as the Servicemen's Readjustment Act of 1944 to address the lack of jobs for soldiers returning from World War II. The legislation provided unemployment income along with low-interest and no-down-payment housing loans, but is better known for continued education and job training. The War Department underestimated the number of servicemen who would take advantage of support for education, and just over two million veterans went to school. The number of students going to college in the US literally doubled overnight. Instantly, the federal government was in the business of supporting higher education through individual students.

This massive influx of new students required colleges to serve twice as many students, many of whom would not have otherwise attended—lacking either the money or scholastic credentials—had it not been for the post war legislation. These staid institutions scrambled to bring on the manpower for managing the money and red tape associated with this flood of federal funds and figure out how to meet the educational needs of students that were unlike any they had served before.

Within a decade, the College Board's College Scholarship Service was born to assist low-income and minority students in obtaining money to go to college. Now called the CSS PROFILE, this format has evolved as one of two fact gathering methods for today's need-based financial aid system. Many elite, private universities use the CSS as the preferred approach for identifying worthy candidates for private, merit-based endowment scholarships.

The Department of Education administers the other format in use today, the Free Application for Student Aid (FAFSA). Any institution of higher education that wants to receive federally funded financial aid money requires students to complete the FAFSA.

The bottom line: since the end of World War II, Americans have come to expect access to higher education regardless of economic circumstances. Programs funded by colleges and the federal government support those expectations and efforts.

The rest of this chapter will show you how these programs work and what you need to know to make the most of them.

Differences in the Formulas

Filing the FAFSA can be more stressful than filing a tax return. But certain private schools want you to file the PROFILE, too. What gives?

All PROFILE schools use the FAFSA to determine which applicants qualify for the federal or state financial aid they administer on their end. When it comes to awarding the school's endowment money, however, the PROFILE schools look more closely at the financial circumstances for each family to determine who gets what. The PROFILE is much more detailed than the FAFSA and asks twice as many questions about family finances.

To further complicate things, colleges that use the PROFILE can choose from hundreds of supplemental questions, meaning your PROFILE calculation won't be the same from college to college. Each school gets to treat our answers differently. This is akin to the Coca-Cola formula: no one knows how the schools that use the CSS Profile calculate the EFC.

The Golden Rule operates here: He who has the gold makes the rules. This is why you must get comfortable working with an EFC range as opposed to an actual number. By the way, it costs nothing to file the FAFSA. The CSS Profile costs $25 for the initial application (a onetime setup fee) and $16 for each additional school.

The table below outlines the assets that must be included in the financial aid formulas and how income and assets are counted. It's important that we understand which items are used in each calculation so if any planning opportunities present themselves we will know where to act to improve our college financing outcome.

	FAFSA Used by all colleges	CSS PROFILE Used by 229 colleges (in addition to the FAFSA)
Bank Accounts	√	√
CDs, Savings Bonds	√	√
529 Plans, Prepaid Tuition Programs	√	√
Education Savings Accounts	√	√
UTMA/Uniform Gifts to Minors Act (UGMA) Accounts	√	√
Vested Stock Options	√	√
Investment Real Estate (real estate that is NOT your primary residence)	√	√
Commodities (gold, silver)	√	√
Nonretirement Investments (stocks, bonds, mutual funds, exchange traded funds [ETFs] that are NOT in an individual retire account [IRA], 401(k), 403(b), etc.)	√	√
Home Equity		√
Nonqualified Annuities (not in an IRA or 401k) or Cash Value in Life Insurance		√ (rarely but in some cases)
Business		√
Farm		√
Parent Income	22%–47%	22%–47%
Student Income	50%	50%
Parent Assets	5.64%	5%
Student Assets	20%	25%

Both formulas consider the number of people supported in the household (including aging parents, stepchildren, etc.), the age of the oldest parent (the formulas shield more of the parents' income and assets as we get older and closer to retirement), and the number of full-time students in college at the same time (recognizing that having more kids in college at the same time poses a financial challenge).

Given how complicated the process is and the need to reveal your financial life to strangers, no one would blame you for not wanting to participate. I meet parents every year that are hesitant to complete the forms, many are opposed to disclosing financial information as a matter of principle. I appreciate the sentiment but must insist you have nothing to lose and everything to gain. Here are a few thoughts to consider:

- Financial aid is a tool that can and should be leveraged. You've paid into the system every year you've paid taxes, and you've earned the right to use it to your advantage.

- Filing for financial aid increases the probability of merit-based aid at schools where your student falls into the top quartile (based on GPA, test scores, and transcript) of students admitted to the freshman class.

- Financial aid can improve your cash flow during college years, allowing you to stay on track for retirement and maintain your current lifestyle.

- You are in no way obligated to take an offer of financial aid. You can accept all, some, or none of what is awarded to your student. Why not give yourself as many options as possible and make an informed decision?

Every family should apply for financial aid, but the reasons for filing will be quite different depending on whether you are an ALWAYS, SOMETIMES, or NEVER family as described in chapter 6.

An ALWAYS family should endure the mind-numbing exercise of filing the forms because a significant amount of the cost of college will be offset by grants and loans made available to you through federal, state, and school related programs. The system was designed for your situation, and you should make use of the help that's being offered. Sadly, it is often those that would benefit the most that are intimidated by the complexity of the FAFSA and CSS Profile process and abandon the effort, costing them dearly in terms of access to funding for college. I urge you to take the time to figure it out or invest in professional assistance for the task. Remember that college is a six-figure investment. The money and time you invest will be well worth the money saved on this critical phase of the project.

SOMETIMES and NEVER households should also take on this administrative challenge because you stand a strong chance of increasing your eligibility for free money because you are opening the financial kimono.

In chapter 9, I'll explain dynamic pricing, but for purposes of this discussion, please realize that like airline passengers and hotel guests, not every student pays the same price. If your student meets the college's enrollment criteria (top 25 percent of students admitted based on GPA, test scores, and transcript), schools will create financial incentives to entice your student to attend. Your job is to make sure your student is considered desirable by that school.

In the wacky world of college today, the fact that you may not need as much financial help for college makes you more attractive for receiving it—provided your student fits a certain profile and the school believes your student will improve their rankings, allowing them to continue to raise their cost of attendance.

Equally important, kids overlapping in college means the EFC is split between them, and each student will be eligible for more financial aid. Said another way, in the years when you have more kids in college, you will likely be eligible for more help from the financial aid system. So it's worth your time and effort to raise your hand.

WHO FILES THE FINANCIAL AID FORMS?

As family structures have changed, so has the filing status for financial aid. College kids don't always come from homes with married parents, and understanding who should complete the forms isn't always straightforward.

Here's a simple rule of thumb: If both parents live in the same house with the student, they file the FAFSA jointly, whether married or not. Same-sex couples may encounter a wrinkle regarding this rule. If they are married, they file jointly. If they are not married but the non-biological parent has adopted his or her partner's child, they file jointly. If they live together, are not married, and the partner has not adopted the child, only the biological parent will complete the FAFSA.

When parents are divorced or separated, the custodial parent completes the FAFSA. A custodial parent for financial aid purposes is the parent the child lived with most during the prior twelve months. If it's a true joint-custody arrangement, most families are best served by having the parent with the least income and least assets (creating a lower EFC) file the form. It's worth noting that it does *not* matter which parent claims the child on his or her tax return or which parent pays child support.

When it comes to the CSS PROFILE, the rules on who files vary by college. Most schools require the noncustodial parent to file several forms too. If the student lives with a legal guardian—an older brother or sister, a grandparent, or an aunt or uncle—the student is considered independent, but there must be a court order to support this status. If guardianship was established by an attorney or merely assigned, or it's a foster parent arrangement, it's not grounds for independent status.

While we are discussing whether a student is considered independent for financial aid purposes, it's interesting to note that back in 1992, the loopholes related to emancipating a child for financial aid purposes were eliminated. Too many families abused the system for the Department of Education to ignore it. Since then, to be considered independent, a student must be able to answer "yes" to at least one of the following questions:

1. Are you twenty-four years of age?

2. Are you married? Or separated?

3. Have you completed a bachelor's degree? And will you be pursuing a master's or doctorate degree?

4. Are you active duty military?

5. Are you a veteran of the US military?

6. Do you have children of your own who rely on you for support?

7. Do you have other dependents (besides spouse or children) who depend on you for half of their support?

8. After age thirteen, were both parents deceased, were you in foster care, or were you a ward of the court?

9. Has a court in your state of legal residence determined you are an emancipated minor or assigned legal guardianship for you to an adult?

10. Are you an unaccompanied youth who is homeless (as determined by the director of an emergency shelter or transitional housing program)?

HIDDEN COST INCREASE

The government adjusts how much parents can shield from a formula based on the age of the oldest parent (according to the income and asset protection allowance tables)[20] each year based on the rules laid out in 1965 by the Higher Education Act. In typical government fashion, they haven't updated the formulas since then, so we are living with the consequences of a seriously outdated approach: Most families have no protection of assets.

---

[20] Edvisors, "Asset Protection Allowance Plummets, Cutting Financial Aid to Middle-Income Students," *The Edvisors Blog*, retrieved October 23, 2016 (https://www.edvisors.com/blog/asset-protection-allowance-plummets-08-2015/).

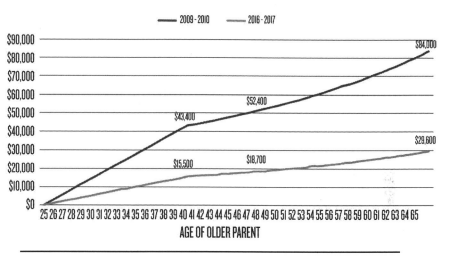

Asset Protection Allowance by Age of Older Parent

─── 2009 - 2010   ⋯⋯ 2016 - 2017

Copyright Edvisors Network, Inc.

Family incomes since 2009 are flat or declining (so there is little to no impact on the income protection calculation), but Social Security benefits have continued to grow. Because the formula used to calculate the allowance is based on the difference between a family's income and average Social Security benefits, we see a shrinking asset protection allowance while college costs continue to outpace any other category of spending in American life.

In plain English, more and more of the money we work so hard to save is exposed to the financial aid formula and drives up our EFC, no matter the age of the oldest parent. We face what amounts to yet another college cost increase, courtesy of Congress being asleep at the wheel.

Most families fall into the SOMETIMES category of financial aid. Some of the grant programs (e.g., Pell Grant or Federal Supplemental Educational Opportunity Grant [FSEOG]) will be made available only to ALWAYS families or households with $50,000 or less in annual income.

Several other programs can benefit a wider range of families. They include the following:

- **TEACH Grant** provides up to $4,000 a year for students who will become teachers specializing in high-demand fields (math and science) and who are willing to work in low-income school districts for four years. This is *not* need based.

- **Iraq and Afghanistan Service Grants** offer up to $5,775 per year for undergraduate students who lost a parent during the Iraq War or the War in Afghanistan. These grants are available for families that qualify due to their circumstances but whose income is too high to qualify for Pell Grants.

- **Work Study** is possible for families making more than $100,000 per year. This program allows student who qualify to work and receive wages *that are not assessed as income in the financial aid calculations* and use that money earned to help pay for school, including direct costs from the university. As you might imagine, these programs are in demand and go quickly, so it's critical that families file their FAFSA as early as possible and accept the offers because work study is awarded on a first-come first-served basis.

- **Federal Direct Loans** are true student loans (responsibility for repayment lies with the student only, and the parents do not cosign) and represent the most used program in the financial aid system. Students, *regardless of their EFC*, qualify for these loans if they are enrolled as at least half-time and have completed a FAFSA. There is no credit score qualification requirement, repayment programs tied to income are available, and loan forgiveness programs exist for certain public service jobs. The interest rate is generally low (2016 rates were 3.76 percent). Once the rate is locked in, it will not change.

- **Subsidized** loans are generally awarded to students whose families report an annual income less than $50,000. The interest that accrues on this loan while the student is in school is paid by the federal government.

- **Unsubsidized** loans are *not* need based (e.g., Mark Zuckerberg's child will qualify). Anyone who completes the FAFSA is eligible to receive these student loans, but the government does not pay the interest during the college years. These loans come with limits:

Freshman Year	$5,500
Sophomore Year	$6,500
Junior Year	$7,500
Senior Year	$7,500
More than four years	$4,000
	(one-time additional loan)

- **Parent PLUS Loans** were created to provide parents with the ability to borrow as a means of bridging the gap because most financial aid packages awarded to families do not meet all the costs of college. Some qualifications for these loans exist, but they are quite liberal. Obligations for these loans cannot be discharged in bankruptcy. Parents may borrow up to the cost of attendance – an amount that is determined by the college. This uncapped nature of the program has given schools free reign to increase their costs, knowing the federal government will make sure parents have access to more money. Far too many parents have discovered the ease of accessing this money can lead to borrowing more than monthly cash flow can actually support. In the event of death or disability, however, the loan will be forgiven.

- **State-Funded Financial Assistance:** State governments and the colleges they support don't have the same advantages that the federal government enjoys. They can't print money. Budget cuts have reduced the funds available for state-supported higher education across the country. Nonetheless, every state offers a variety of scholarships worth considering.

A quick trip to the Financial Aid in Your State page of the National Association of Student Financial Aid Administrators site will show you what might be available. States require you to file the FAFSA because they use it to evaluate every potential candidate for state-administered funds. Many of them require scholarship applications above and beyond the FAFSA form. More money almost always requires more forms to complete. Understand that most states use their precious financial aid dollars to keep the best and brightest within their borders and ask out-of-state residents to foot the bill for the home team.

Interestingly, I've noticed a sea change in recent years. State universities want to raise their rankings and diversify the student body, so they have created enticing incentives for smart, out-of-state students. It all boils down to money.

Attracting smarter, wealthier kids (based on GPA, test scores, and FAFSA) raises state university rankings. An out-of-state student, even one who receives a lucrative incentive to attend, most often pays more than an in-state student. Out-of-state students are therefore profitable, so it makes sense to entice those students to join the incoming freshman class as the University of Alabama has done.

The University of Alabama's dominance on the football field is legendary. The Crimson Tide's success comes from the aggressive recruiting around the country. Last year's recruiting class included 27 players from 15 states—many of whom were four- and five-star prospects.

What most people don't know is that the University of Alabama takes the same intense approach when recruiting top out-of-state students. The school has at least 30 full-time admissions officers spread throughout the country. And they come armed with generous merit-based scholarship packages to lure high-achieving students to their school.

It wasn't always so. In the late 1990's, the University of Alabama's admissions office had become complacent. While the admissions staff did some recruiting, the staff generally expected students to be interested in the school because of its long history and status as a flagship university. Heading into the new century, the university, which marketed itself mainly on athletic programs and social traditions, was having trouble attracting top students.

Enter Robert E. Witt, the former business school dean at the University of Texas at Austin and president of the University of Texas at Arlington. Upon taking the presidency of the University of Alabama in 2003, he laid down a challenge to the admissions office: to "recruit top student scholars with the same fervor as top athletic prospects, and look beyond the state's borders to find them."

In the years since, the university has been remarkably successful in attracting nonresident students. Today, in fact, there are more out-of-state students on campus that in-state ones—a strategy that has helped the school weather large-scale budget cuts from the state. Admissions officers at several public universities in different parts of the country said in interviews recently that Alabama has been actively recruiting in their home states. "Alabama has recruiters everywhere," a top official from a competing flagship university stated. "It's really played well for them."

The University of Alabama is not alone in its aggressive pursuit of out-of-state students. Over the past two decades, there has been a fundamental shift in the admissions practices of many public four-year colleges and universities. Stung by sharp state budget cuts at the same time they are seeking greater prestige, these universities are increasingly pitted against one another, fiercely competing for students that they most desire: the best, the brightest, and those wealthy enough to pay full freight. And they are using a large share of their institutional dollars—money that could be going to students that truly need it—to entice these generally privileged students to their schools.

Excerpt from *The Out-of-State Arms Race:*
How Public Universities Use Merit Aid
to Recruit Nonresident Students
Stephen Burd, May 2015[21]

REGIONAL RECIPROCITY PROGRAMS

To provide access to programs that are not homegrown, neighboring states have come together to allow students from out of state to benefit from degree programs they couldn't get at their state university. For example, Nevada has only two state schools: University of Nevada Las Vegas and University of Nevada Reno. Neither offered a doctorate of veterinary medicine, so students had no choice but to cross the state line in search of that degree program.

The Western Undergraduate Exchange (WUE; pronounced "woo-E") swoops in to address that disparity: fifteen western states agree to provide tuition discounts to students from those states that choose to attend a participating school *where they would be considered out of state.* The schools agree to offer discounted costs to candidates who meet their criteria.

---

[21] Stephen Burd, *The Out-of-State Student Arms Race: How Public Universities Use Merit Aid to Recruit Nonresident Students* (Washington, DC: New America, 2015). Retrieved October 23, 2016 (https://www.dropbox.com/s/zba6kqgsee3r6ll/Out-of-State-Student-Arms-Race.pdf?dl=0).

Most regions of the country offer these "reciprocity discounts," and they can offer substantial savings for the family. These days, it's no longer limited to programs that aren't available in state. There isn't usually a box we can check on the admissions application and every school applies the principles of the program differently, but an above-average student applying to a neighboring out-of-state school should inquire as to how to qualify for discounts if they are available.

West:	——————	Western Undergraduate Exchange
South:	——————	Academic Common Market
Midwest:	——————	Midwest Higher Education Compact
New England:	——————	New England Board of Higher Education

Now that you understand who should file and what is available, the final critical item you need to know is when to file.

PRIOR-PRIOR YEAR TAX REPORTING

The school year straddles two different tax years, a situation that creates confusion and frustration for most of us who already view filing our taxes as being as much fun as dragging nails across a chalkboard.

A recent change in the financial aid filing deadline (now in October each year) and the decision to use the income tax results from two years prior to filing (the genesis of the catchy "prior-prior" title) means we need to plan *much earlier* than in past years for funding college. We won't feel the full impact of this change for a few years, but schools will inevitably drive our behavior in the direction of combining early action or early decision applications with earlier award letters so families will make their decisions well in advance of the traditional National Decision Day on May 1. Because schools will have families' financial information earlier and not get bogged down with delays related to unfiled tax returns (the whole rationale for using tax returns from two years back), they can manage their enrollment more efficiently and effectively.

But it means parents need to start their EFC and cash flow planning beginning when their oldest child is a sophomore in high school. This will come as a *big* surprise to many families in the next few years. To avoid the surprise, confirm your dates in the table on the following page.

	Start Year	Academic Year 1	Academic Year 2	Tax Year
Child 1	2017	2017	2018	2015
		2018	2019	2016
		2019	2020	2017
		2020	2021	2018
		2021	2022	2019
Child 2	2018	2018	2019	2016
		2019	2020	2017
		2020	2021	2018
		2021	2022	2019
		2022	2023	2020
Child 3	2021	2021	2022	2019
		2022	2023	2020
		2023	2024	2021
		2024	2025	2022
		2025	2026	2023
Child 4	2023	2023	2024	2021
		2024	2025	2022
		2025	2026	2023
		2026	2027	2024
		2027	2028	2025

APPLY FOR FINANCIAL AID

Start Planning Early

Parents need to do any asset repositioning or tax planning beginning in January of the student's sophomore year in high school—much earlier than in the past. The "base year" sets the tone from a financial aid perspective, so parents want to do the heavy lifting that tax year.

At almost every financial aid night I've attended at high schools, the presenters stand on stage and insist that no one should pay to have their FAFSA or CSS Profile prepared. When parents ask questions about filing the forms, the presenters admit that they don't know the answers to the questions, nor are they qualified to address the concerns raised.

More than 60 percent of tax returns filed each year are completed with the assistance of professional tax preparation services, and 96 percent of parents with college-bound students have tax returns professionally prepared.[22] Filing the FAFSA and CSS Profile is more complicated than filing a tax return, so I don't follow the logic that this is a do-it-yourself exercise. In fact, I would argue there is much more at stake for your family.

And the policy makers and college administrators who run this show can alter the college financing landscape overnight in big ways, as we've seen with the prior-prior tax year filing, and in small ways, as with annual tuition increases. These changes impact how and when you plan for college financing, what you can afford, and ultimately where your student should apply for admission. Having spent more than a decade dealing with the painstaking minutiae involved with optimizing aid eligibility, and understanding that the landscape can change in the blink

---

[22] Financial Aid for Tax Preparers website (http://financialaidfortaxpreparers.com/).

of an eye, I can assure you, I will definitely pay for assistance in filing the forms for my son when the time comes.

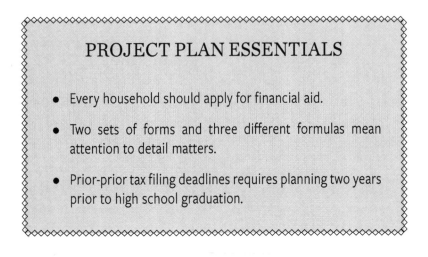

PROJECT PLAN ESSENTIALS

- Every household should apply for financial aid.

- Two sets of forms and three different formulas mean attention to detail matters.

- Prior-prior tax filing deadlines requires planning two years prior to high school graduation.

CHAPTER EIGHT

ASSESS RETIREMENT

READINESS

AND CALCULATE

CASH FLOW

FOR COLLEGE

Prior to take off, flight attendants remind passengers to put on their oxygen mask in the event of an emergency. They make a point of telling passengers, "**If you are traveling with a small child or someone else who requires assistance, put your mask on first and then assist the other person**." Although we've grown complacent about the instructions, we should take the message to heart: You can't help anyone else unless you can help yourself.

When it comes to paying for our children's education, we should be reciting the flight attendant script morning, noon, and night. If we're not on the right trajectory to fund our retirement, introducing college to the flight plan is not likely to result in an on-time arrival. Most of us, unfortunately, aren't paying attention. We think we'll get our kids through school first and then get serious about saving for our own retirement.[23] Our kids can get loans and scholarships for school; we will not get them for retirement. The world has changed, and we need to change with it.

The first iPhone was released on June 29, 2007.

I almost can't remember how we accomplished anything before that summer. "Smart Phone" seems so inadequate a description for holding the world in our hands. But once we understood what it could do for us and recognized the blessings and the curse it represents, we integrated it into our daily lives and have never looked back.

Amazingly, there was no real training for this thing that has come to dominate our daily lives. We picked it up and figured out how to use it on the fly, continually learning how to make the most of it. And once we feel as if we really understand how it works, they trot out an upgrade, a change, a better/faster/different version for us to master.

And we take it right in stride. We have no choice. Adapt or be left behind.

---

[23]   Lee Barney, "Child's College Education Puts Retirement Savings on the Back Burner," *Plan Sponsor*, June 15, 2016 (http://www.plansponsor.com/Childs-College-Education-Puts-Retirement-Savings-on-the-Back-Burner/).

I'm begging you to bring that flexible, adaptable attitude of acceptance to this next topic. Abandon your preconceived notions and nostalgia for what's worked in the past. Look forward and embrace the blessings that this new approach has to offer because you will be rewarded for adapting (or be punished for refusing to change).

If we don't know what it's going to take to retire and support ourselves later in life, how can we possibly make an informed decision about what we're willing to invest in our children's education? You need to understand that time and compounding interest are your greatest allies when it comes to supporting your future lifestyle. When you disrupt the compounding process, you will end up with a less-than-favorable outcome and likely, not the one you were expecting.

Contrary to popular belief, good college planning *begins* with retirement planning. Once retirement goals have been established, you can back into formulating a college budget. Any other approach is like borrowing money for your kitchen remodel only to discover—after the work's been done—that you can't afford to make the monthly payments on that borrowed money. You can't rip the white porcelain farm sink out and return it for a refund. Parents launch themselves into the college project every year, only to discover they have overextended themselves.

We humans tend to think along a chronological time line and progression of life: get married, buy a house, have some kids, send them to college, and retire. Sequence planning neglects the power of time and uninterrupted compounding. Financial literacy is reaching a new low,[24] so it's no wonder most Americans

---

[24]   FINRA Investor Education Foundation 2015 survey, accessed February 17, 2017 (http://www.usfinancialcapability.org/results.php?region=US).

aren't on track to support themselves in retirement or maintain their current standard of living. Although most of us have never received any formal education or training about how money works in our lives, we must understand one thing: When it comes to funding our children's college, we need to write our final chapter first then work backward.

Retirement is a distant and theoretical concept for most people. College, on the other hand, is more like a freight train picking up momentum and heading right at us. When suddenly confronted with the overwhelming reality of college costs, parents take action. Typically, they look to accessible assets first and spend those to meet the initial costs. Then, discovering that those won't get the job done, they evaluate where they can cut back and redirect money toward college. A short note here about why we do this? Something like this: It makes sense. We want what's best for our children, we suffer from peer pressure, and we figure we can always make up the time and money later.

Again, the well runs dry. As stress and panic take root, parents look to financial aid and discover they don't qualify for as much as they'd hoped. This is where desperation and debt kick in. Parents resemble hikers who took the wrong trail: dazed and confused after expending energy in the wrong places, dehydrated, depleted, and in need of rescue.

Today's college education is a cash flow challenge, not a savings challenge.

This is the phase of life when getting serious about being efficient with our money comes sharply into focus. Detailed cash flow planning can help us find money we are losing, unknowingly and unnecessarily, and bring it back for both college and retirement. Rarely can we do this on our own. We're too close to our own situation to see the opportunities. We need an objective, detached perspective to look at things in a different way.

We all have deeply held beliefs about how money works in our life. We need a patient and experienced counselor who is willing to challenge us, educate us, and guide us to a solution that makes sense based on our facts and circumstances, our goals and time lines. Often, the solutions will seem unconventional. They may not match what we hear on CNBC or talk radio, from our brother-in-law, or from a coworker.

Again, this is a project, not a product. The FedEx driver is not going to drop off a box labeled "financial peace of mind." You want to collaborate with an architect to design a blueprint for your future. In any ambitious project, what is outlined on paper must be adapted during construction. The permit process changes, the materials that arrive on the job site don't match what we selected from the glossy brochure, or the subcontractor doesn't show up on time.

We need a *big picture* plan we can understand and stick with, knowing it will evolve during implementation. Essentially, we want to optimize what we have without allowing money to evaporate from our savings and investment accounts. Think of this as the traffic pattern approach to laying out your new kitchen. At the end of the day, we want a kitchen that looks great, works well, and doesn't break the bank.

This part of the equation is actually pretty simple, which is not to be confused with being easy.

If we're serious about our financial future, we must answer these four questions:[25]

1. What **rate of return** do we have to earn on our savings and investment dollars to be able to retire at our current standard of living and have our money last as long as we do?

2. How much do we **need to save** on a monthly or annual basis to be able to retire and enjoy the same lifestyle we live now through our life expectancy?

3. Doing what we're doing now, **how long will we have to work** to become financially independent and enjoy all our nonworking years?

4. If we don't do anything differently than we're doing today, what level of **downsizing** will we need to embrace to have our money last as long as we do?

Sending our kids to college introduces a fifth question that must be asked and answered:

5. How does **funding our children's education** impact the answers to the previous four questions?

Answering these questions can be done in less than twenty minutes.[26] If we're organized, it takes only ten minutes. Really.

---

[25] These questions were created by Don Blanton of MoneyTrax (http://www.moneytrax.com/).

[26] The tools to answer these questions are available to financial advisers who license them from MoneyTrax (http://www.moneytrax.com/).

Yet, most parents don't even begin to think about this until after the kids get through college.

Crafting answers we're going to like will take commitment and some out-of-the-box solutions. The simple message is this: Get firmly focused on what it takes to reach retirement and then back into the amount of money you can invest in college.

Listen to people who have already reached the "retirement summit":

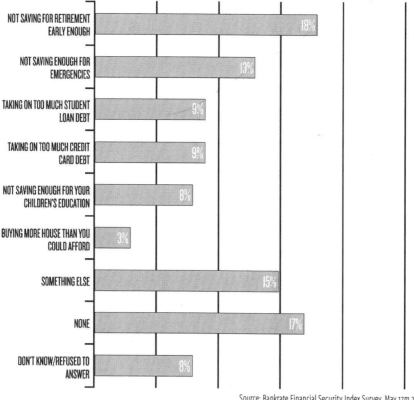

WHAT WOULD YOU SAY IS YOUR BIGGEST FINANCIAL REGRET?

NOT SAVING FOR RETIREMENT EARLY ENOUGH	19%
NOT SAVING ENOUGH FOR EMERGENCIES	13%
TAKING ON TOO MUCH STUDENT LOAN DEBT	9%
TAKING ON TOO MUCH CREDIT CARD DEBT	9%
NOT SAVING ENOUGH FOR YOUR CHILDREN'S EDUCATION	8%
BUYING MORE HOUSE THAN YOU COULD AFFORD	3%
SOMETHING ELSE	15%
NONE	17%
DON'T KNOW/REFUSED TO ANSWER	8%

Source: Bankrate Financial Security Index Survey, May 17m 2016
Results May Not Ttotal 100% Due to Rounding

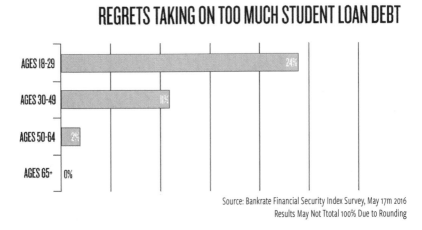

REGRETS TAKING ON TOO MUCH STUDENT LOAN DEBT

Source: Bankrate Financial Security Index Survey, May 17m 2016
Results May Not Ttotal 100% Due to Rounding

Once we've answered the four critical questions regarding our future lifestyle, we can focus on our real-world or "working family contribution," which is the amount of money we can actually afford to put toward our children's college education. Todd Fothergill, president of Strategies for College,[27] coined the term "working family contribution", bringing sanity and sensibility to the rather outlandish idea that anyone can assign an "expected" amount of money to our household for educating our kids.

Understanding how much we can afford to invest in college—all kids, all years—means backing into a number. It's an exercise in thorough and detailed cash flow planning that *needs to start no later than our oldest student's sophomore year.* Because of the change to prior-prior tax reporting, we create the baseline for financial aid during the tax year that begins in January of our

---

[27] You can find out more about Todd Fothergill and Strategies for College Inc. at http://www.strategiesforcollege.com/.

oldest child's sophomore year. That's an ideal time not only to do income tax planning, but also overall cash flow planning for college.

Which brings us to the single most important element of the parent project plan: POOP. The **parent-out-of-p**ocket score. My colleague, Stuart Siegel, a nationally recognized expert in financial aid, admissions, and school selection and the founder of the College Family Care Center, coined this term to help parents understand what they can actually afford before the student applies for college.

Flight attendant. Oxygen mask. You first.

Your Affordability Review & Workable Family Contribution™

	Data
FUNDING COLLEGE - The Workable Family Contribution (WFC)	
Annual Cash Flow For College	9,600
Maximum Parent PLUS Loan Allowance (Over this time period) - See Note 1	66,225
Annual Cash Flow Needed to Service Parent College Loans - See Note 2	
Parent Savings & Investments (For This Student)	20,000
Student Savings and Investments	10,000
From Student Summer Job (increased by 5% annually)	2,000
From Unsubsidized Private Student Loan (ENTER TOTAL) - See Note 3	
From Unsubsidized Federal Student Loan (Enter 1 TO TOGGLE ON/OFF)	
Based on data provided above - You can afford these annual amounts ---->	
What you can afford compared to your EFC (FM)	$31,906
What you can afford compared to your EFC (IM)	$27,283

When EFC > WFC, you will need to either:

1) reallocate your resources

2) further reduce the EFC

3) choose colleges that fit your WFC or if appropriate

4) select colleges that have non-need based merit funding

Year 1	Year 2	Year 3	Year 4
$9,600	$9,600	$9,600	$9,600
$16,556	$16,556	$16,556	$16,556
-(2,400)	-(4,800)	-(7,200)	-(9,600)
$5,000	$5,000	$5,000	$5,000
$2,500	$2,500	$2,500	$2,500
$2,000	$,2100	$2,205	$2,315
$ -	$ -	$ -	$ -
$ -	$ -	$ -	$ -
$33,256	$30,956	$28,661	$26,372
$1,350	-($950)	-($3,245)	-($5,534)
$5,973	$3,673	$1,378	-($911)

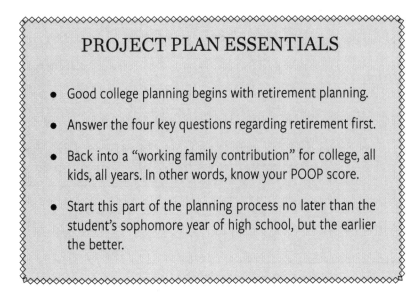

PROJECT PLAN ESSENTIALS

- Good college planning begins with retirement planning.

- Answer the four key questions regarding retirement first.

- Back into a "working family contribution" for college, all kids, all years. In other words, know your POOP score.

- Start this part of the planning process no later than the student's sophomore year of high school, but the earlier the better.

PART III:

THE FAMILY

Select Right Fit Colleges

Assess Scholarship Options

Compare Award Offers

Transition Successfully

Anyone can take your money and your life in their hands and not be accountable.

—PEAKFREAKS.COM REGARDING MT. EVEREST MOUNTAINEERING GUIDE PROGRAMS

Climbing Mt. Everest is not a spur of the moment decision, physically or financially. This project requires rigorous preparation and a deliberate plan of action to secure permission to ascend five and a half miles into the jet stream, carry sixty-five pounds of gear in increasingly thin air with ever-changing weather conditions in less than three hours.

Serious enthusiasts are encouraged to begin their physical training several months to three years before departing for Kathmandu, Nepal. The cost to risk your life and reach the summit can exceed $100,000. You must get yourself to a remote part of the globe, buy a pricey permit for admission to the mountain, pay for guides and acclimation courses, as well as rent tents, communication devices, and oxygen tanks. All of this in hopes that Mother Nature and your own mental and physical stamina will allow you to survive the trek.

Climbing Mt. Everest is a project that requires a plan. It is an endeavor that has a definite start and end. Once the climber arrives home safe and sound, the project is over.

College is a project, too. Most families don't realize that their "college" project starts when the student enters high school, but they do understand that it ends when the student graduates from college. Getting in, getting through, and getting an education from college does attempt (and achieve) something that hasn't been done before.

For most families, college becomes an actual project when the student and parents come together and put their respective component parts together, typically the summer between the student's junior and senior year of high school.

Up until this time, the student has been busy doing high school, building college credentials, becoming self-aware, developing a mindset for the future, and preparing to apply to colleges. The parents have been—or should have been—getting their financial house in order, estimating their Expected Family Contribution (EFC), answering the four critical questions about their future lifestyle, identifying their cash flow for college, and preparing to file for financial aid.

Now it's time for these separate efforts to merge. The student and the parents begin to work directly as a team. This is the phase of the project plan that can make or break the outcome for everyone. It's also the phase where many families make expensive mistakes that you can avoid.

In the world of project management, you have a project sponsor (Mom and Dad) and a project manager (student). The project sponsor is responsible for defining the scope and time line of the project, as well as securing the financing and overall resources for the project. The sponsor is not concerned with the day-to-day running of the project. That's the responsibility of the project manager. Because of the scope and long-term impact of the college project, some families hire a senior project manager that is responsible for making sure all the who, what, when, and how are taken care of for them. That's the role I find myself in these days. It's my job to understand what the family wants to accomplish as it relates to college and help them figure out what needs to be done to make it happen. The timeline, the tools, the team of people that can bring it in on time and on budget - that's what they hire me to handle.

NEVER PAY RETAIL FOR COLLEGE

Let's face it, some of us are better at managing projects than others. Half the battle is understanding what needs to be done, by when, and who's accountable. In this phase of the college project plan, families should focus on strategic school selection, recognizing how and where scholarships (free money) will play a role in their overall funding strategy, understanding the award appeal process, and preparing to transition successfully into this next phase of family life.

CHAPTER NINE

SELECT RIGHT-FIT COLLEGES

As an A-list member of the Rapid Rewards program for Southwest Airlines, I enjoy the probability of a seat closer to the cockpit, storing my carry-on bag in a luggage bin (for no added fee, I might add!), and not having to sit in a middle seat. But I also know that the people sitting next to me, although departing from the same airport and landing at the same destination, are not paying the same price for their seat—some paid more, some paid less. And we're all getting the same peanuts, soda, and closet-like bathroom experience.

Dynamic pricing, also known as yield management, is the adjustment of prices depending on demand, supply, or competition. American Airlines introduced this practice in the early 1980s in response to the threat posed by discount airline People's Express. The hotel industry began to use similar tactics in the early 2000s. In the trucking industry, it's called backhaul—hauling new cargo, for a price, from where you just dropped off your load, so you don't drive back empty.

Any business trying to make a profit wants to optimize the laws of supply and demand as it relates to their inventory. Businesses want to match a paying customer with something they sell. In some instances, they discount prices rather than miss a revenue opportunity. When demand is high, they can charge a premium price. It's a moving target and requires data integration, slice-and-dice reporting capabilities, statistical analysis, and a willingness to harness all that data in an efficient and effective manner.

With airlines, it's seats. With hotels, it's beds. With colleges, it's classrooms.

Enrollment management in higher education emerged in the 1970s. The wave of "buyers" created after World War II had run its course, forcing admissions departments to transition from keeping out the unworthy to attracting the most desirable students. The role of buyers and sellers had flipped. Suddenly, schools accustomed to turning kids away found themselves working to make sure their dorms and classes were full. For the first time, for-profit institutions—skilled in matching eager students with federal financial aid—proved a formidable competitor for increasingly scarce students.

Colleges implemented pricing and financial aid strategies to attract and retain the kind of students they wanted for each incoming freshman class: academically, demographically, and financially. No two schools approach enrollment management the same way. In today's hypercompetitive education marketplace, colleges have discovered the art and science of an analytical, data-driven approach. They want to find students who are likely to raise admissions standards (along with rankings in annual magazines), graduate on time, pay the optimal price, and contribute to the alumni endowment campaign in twenty years.

SAS, a business analytics software and service company, touts the work it did at the University of Oregon (UO). The goal was to "find out if UO's merit aid was being used effectively to boost enrollment rates." SAS helped the Ducks develop a financial aid simulator so the admissions department could redesign its merit aid program to recruit better students more effectively. These tools allowed administrators to learn how much merit aid was needed in a financial aid package to attract high-achieving, in-state students to their school. As parents, we need to fight back by using our own tools to find those colleges that are most likely to provide us with meaningful discounts.

In my years of helping parents avoid paying retail for college, if I had to boil the entire project plan down to one critical component, it would be creating the college list. Determining where a student applies makes the single biggest impact on the overall cost of college—positive or negative—because if we are sending our sons or daughters to a school strictly for the prestige or reputation, we will be paying retail. If we take the time and do the work, we can spend less money providing an education that actually serves our student better.

Business Insider published a report in February 2015 called "The 50 Most Underrated Colleges in America."[28] The authors cross-referenced *US News and World Report* college rankings with the college salary report from PayScale, which is in the business of telling us what we're worth in the employment marketplace by linking individuals and businesses to the largest salary profile database in the world and evaluated colleges and universities based on the mid-career salaries of their graduates. The results are fascinating, and many of the top-ranked schools may not be names you immediately recognize. The schools that receive top-name billing in annual lists are not necessarily the ones that will deliver the best or most affordable education. When your student's college list contains only name-brand schools, your options are limited, and the financial implications could be crippling.

Frank Bruni, New York Times op-ed columnist and author of *Where You Go Is Not Who You'll Be*, talks about the dangers of being seduced by name-brand schools in an interview appearing on Lisa Hefferman's blog, Grown and Flown.

> My point is that those advantages [networking in an elite school] are nullified, and maybe even reversed, if a child buys too fully into the idea of them and shortchanges the quality and energy of the work done in college, and that's a danger of too much belief in, and talk about, the importance of a school's name. The danger is that you think admission is all and experience is secondary.[29]

[28]   Melissa Stanger, Emmie Martin, and Andy Kiersz, "The 50 Most Underrated Colleges in America," *Business Insider*, January 28, 2015 (http://www.businessinsider.com/most-underrated-colleges-in-america-2015-1).
[29]   Frank Bruni in interview with Lisa Heffernan author and co-founder of Grown and Flown in interview with "Does it Matter Where You Go to College?" http://grownandflown.com/where-you-go-to-college/ accessed February 5, 2017.

The problem isn't only that you'll pay retail, but the real possibility that you'll pay retail and your student won't get the benefit of the cost.

I can't imagine making a six-figure investment decision with little or no knowledge of the probable outcome, but it happens every year when kids apply to college. Why? The foundation hasn't been laid. The money talk never took place. The context for making a good decision was never created. And the family didn't understand how to qualify for the discounted rate in the college's dynamic pricing model. We don't have a framework for this. Our parents didn't have to approach the project this way, so why would we? Like frogs in a pot of boiling water, we haven't noticed the danger we're in.

The high school senior, who's held up his end of the bargain and is accepted to the name-brand school, is heartbroken when he discovers he can't attend because the family can't make the payments. Or worse yet, the student is accepted, and Mom and Dad are too embarrassed to tell their child they can't afford it. The parents then go into debt and end up working an extra ten years into what would have been their retirement.

Kathy, a conflicted parent, in just that situation explained that her oldest daughter, Hannah, had spoken with a recent graduate of a name-brand school who was working a booth at the high school's college fair. Hannah had felt excited and checked on the possibility of attending that school with her guidance counselor. He had told her it was definitely a reach school, but if she applied early, it would improve her chances.

Before Kathy and her husband, Steven, knew what was happening, Hannah had been accepted. They felt they had no other choice but to go through with it. This is how Hannah came to be attending an expensive private school back East.

Hannah had the grades and test scores to get in, but just barely. She applied early decision and was accepted. Applying early decision demonstrated Hannah's serious interest. Kathy and Steven made enough money to fall smack-dab in the middle of the SOMETIMES category of financial aid. From the college's perspective, this was an attractive family—financially—so they offered Hannah admission.

They were in no-man's-land. They made too much money to qualify for a lot of need-based aid. Plus, this school was overflowing with applications from smart kids, so they offered no discounts. Hannah was thrilled to have been accepted, but Kathy and Steven were panic-stricken once they understood the actual cost. They felt obligated to comply with the terms of early decision.

They accepted the offer.

To make matters worse, Hannah's younger sister, Emily, was only two years behind. If they were already digging themselves into a hole on Hannah's college tuition, how on earth could they add Emily's education to this hot mess?

The good news is they survived this situation and turned it around by having Emily take a more strategic approach to her college applications. As parents, we try to treat our kids equally and not favor one over the other. Imagine what went through these parents' minds. They believed they had to provide Emily with the same kind of college education as Hannah, but they were thinking same cost, not same value.

We identified schools where Emily would fall into the top quartile of the incoming freshman class. By combining a small stipend for playing soccer with a larger, merit-based academic award, we found a school for Emily that offered a great fit—academically, athletically, socially, and financially. Emily never felt as if she were getting short-changed—quite the contrary. Because she was involved in the process and took ownership over which schools she applied to, she was thrilled with her choice. Kathy and Steven went from being super stressed to totally relieved, knowing they wouldn't have to work until they were seventy-five to make college a reality for both of their girls.

As parents, we can and should know how much money a college is going to cost *before* our kids complete the application. If a certain school isn't within the parameters we've established because of our circumstances, the student shouldn't apply. It's OK for kids to apply to schools they haven't heard of, or that their friends haven't heard of, or that most kids from their high school class aren't attending. What is the "success criteria" for your student? Where are they most likely to succeed, thrive, and graduate in four years? Research potential schools with these questions top of mind. Just because you can be admitted to a school doesn't mean you should accept the offer.

It's simple, really. It is the theory of relativity put into action.

Apply to colleges and universities where it is likely your student will land in the top 25 percent of the freshman class—hence, the "relativity." It's how he or she measures up relative to his or her peer group at that school. You can determine this by looking at the three critical components for admission: unweighted GPA, ACT or SAT score, and high school transcript.[30] This is one area where logic and facts should win over marketing and emotion.

---

[30]   Visit us at CenterforCollegeSolutions.com and download a strategic college list.

For your student, typical selection criteria should include the size of the school, the distance from home or extended family, availability of desired major(s), the climate, the sports culture, reputation, internship opportunities, religious affiliation, access to faculty, four-year graduation rates, percentage of graduates employed within six months of graduation, opportunities for advanced study (master's or doctorate), the Greek system, and job placement statistics.

The best practice? Match the student's qualifications with the schools; filter the schools where he or she shows up in the top quartile by the criteria you've established. That way, you end up with schools that are likely to offer meaningful affordability options in addition to the other important elements on your list.

One of the parents I worked with closely had this to say about college selection:

> *The third time's the charm. As college-educated parents of four children, going to college was not an option; it was an expectation. Because of the crazy, rising costs of college and inaccurate information we had at the time, we believed we were limited to a public, in-state university. The idea of our children attending an out-of-state public or private school seemed out of the question.*
>
> *Our firstborn attended an in-state, public university. Our second child received an appointment to the United States Merchant Marine Academy. For our third child, we followed the College Rx that Beth provided.*
>
> *Our third child wanted to attend college out of state to study at a top journalism school. To prepare, she persevered through a rigorous two final years in high school. We didn't realize that it was possible, but soon learned that our daughter*

could choose from a variety of schools—if we followed the plan. Our daughter applied to several colleges based on her interest in journalism and her connection with the professors in the department after several school visits, proximity to home, and Greek life. The list included a variety of schools including in state, out of state, public, and private. We learned that smaller, private schools have endowments that offer more scholarship dollars to prospective students with less-than-stellar accomplishments.

Our daughter ended up with two great choices accompanied by incredible financial aid packages. Both were out of state and private. She attended the University of Denver on a $39,000 scholarship, which made the cost of attending a private, out-of-state college over $7,000 less per year than our in-state public university. She is beyond thrilled, and so are we. Finding the right fit for the right price is a reality, not an illusion.

As we complete the victory lap and reflect, we are amazed at how much we didn't know and how flawed our thinking was at the time. We learned new things and became smarter parents all because of the intervention we received. From beginning to end, we were supported by a knowledgeable team of experts who led us through a proven plan to find the best college fit for the right price. With timely guidance and effective coaching, we felt empowered to examine the college selection process equipped with a new set of glasses.

Our best advice: Don't wait until your third child to figure this out. We are forever grateful to Beth and her team of experts for providing the encouragement and structure to lead us through this incredibly complex process.

—Joni B.

Even better, her daughter Laney shared the following with me:

Working with Beth and her team helped me navigate the bumpy, twisting turns on the road to college. They helped me narrow my options by giving me a report that took fifteen to twenty colleges and universities I was interested in (and even some I hadn't looked at but could have been of interest to me) and placed them side by side for comparison. It included things like how many students attend, the student-to-faculty ratio, graduation rates, average GPAs, average standardized test scores, cost of attendance, expected family contributions, and out-of-pocket costs. This breakdown was extremely helpful when comparing the schools because it allowed me to rule out ones that were too big, too small, or too expensive for my family to afford, among other reasons.

Additionally, Beth and her team helped my family and me realize that private, out-of-state tuition was not as high and unattainable as we thought it would be but rather, the opposite. Because private institutions receive more endowment money, they can hand out large scholarships more frequently than a state school. Beth and her team helped us figure this out, and for a third child in a family of four, financial and merit scholarship dollars were my ticket into college. They helped us file the FAFSA and complete the CSS Profile, which was very helpful considering I didn't know how to do those things.

Beth and her team were there to help us throughout the entire college application process, and this experience was so valuable for us. I would not be attending my university without them, and I will be forever grateful for all the advice, answers, expertise, and guidance they provided.

—Laney B.

PROJECT PLAN ESSENTIALS

- Theory of relativity: apply to schools likely to offer us a discount based on our student's GPA, test scores, and high school curriculum (in the top 25 percent *relative* to his or her peer group at that school).

- Create a strategic college list based on our success criteria, not magazine rankings or name-brand recognition.

- Only apply to colleges we know we can afford.

CHAPTER TEN

ASSESS
SCHOLARSHIP
OPTIONS

❝We decided years ago that we'd invest in the kids' activities while they were living here at home—you know, club soccer, summer camp programs, tutoring, and all that kind of stuff. We planned to help them a little for college, but we expected them to work and get scholarships like we did. Our parents didn't do much for us as far as college was concerned, and we turned out just fine."

Amelia and Marty were totally comfortable with this approach to sending their kids to college—until I estimated their Expected Family Contribution (EFC) and explained how things worked nowadays.

"If he can get only $5,500 in student loans his first year, where's the rest of the money going to come from?" asked Amelia in total disbelief.

"We don't have that kind of money just sitting around," Marty chimed in. "He'll just have to buckle down and get some scholarships."

Fortunately, we were able to develop a plan that incorporated student loans, but also showed Amelia and Marty how much they would have to contribute and where it would come from without putting them behind for retirement.

In the software development world, the gap between what has been proven to work and what software architects hope to achieve is called vaporware (because it doesn't exist yet). They pencil in a placeholder with the caption, "The great miracle happens here." It's an optimistic way of suggesting they'll figure out a solution before the release deadline. In many households, the idea of students receiving scholarship money is the great miracle that will provide the resources for our kids to get in and complete college.

Few elements of the college project plan are as misunderstood as scholarships. Substantial resources are available for students to access, but knowing where they are, who controls the purse strings, and how to get them is important.

First, parents need to understand the three categories of scholarships:

1. Institutional (colleges and universities)

2. Government (federal and state)

3. Private (corporate and community)

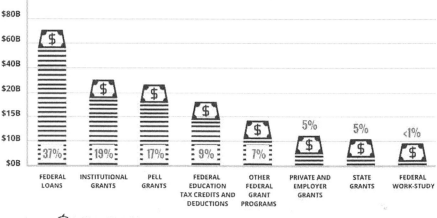

Source: CollegeBoard

Total $185.1 billion for 2012-13 academic year

INSTITUTIONAL

The most significant scholarship money—free money that does not need to be paid back—comes from the schools themselves. It is distributed at the discretion of the university, based largely on the merits of the student—academic, athletic, musical, or otherwise. Universities invest significant time, money, and personnel to raise and manage their endowment funds. They administer those dollars to attract a student body that perpetuates their mission.

Strategic methods of awarding scholarship dollars result in administering gifts to more recipients, and often the awards are lower. For example, a $20,000 scholarship split into four equal parts attracts a higher number of smart, wealthy kids and raises the school's rankings. The colleges have learned how to stretch their dollars to attract the kind of students they want; the key is to be the kind of student they want.

It's no wonder that student bodies at most colleges look like a demographic barbell: smart kids from low-income households weighted equally with smart kids from affluent households. What's missing in this equation are average students and kids from middle-income families. Colleges use federal need-based financial aid to address the needs of the low-income population. They also leverage their own endowment funds to entice smart kids from families that can afford to pay their constantly accelerating rates. The big part of the bell curve—the SOMETIMES folks who represent most US households—have to work harder to make the system work for them. Because so few understand how the system works and whom it favors, they end up paying retail for college.

If we allow ourselves to look at colleges and universities that are not at the top of every ranking report, we will find that our students will be warmly embraced and financially enticed to attend. Increased scholarship dollars will appear, and we will turn the financial road block that college can be into more of a speed bump.

Miller Case Study

The Miller family set aside a fixed amount of money for their daughter to attend college. She was a brilliant student and had earned the highest SAT scores in the state for several years, making her a highly sought-after student. A handful of nationally recognized schools offered her a spot in the freshman class, but she attended an excellent school in the Midwest that no one in her high school knew existed. She chose it because the school awarded her a sizable merit-based scholarship—the largest they make available to any student. With that, the money her parents had saved, and some additional third-party scholarships she had earned, she was able to get an incredible education and have money waiting for her upon earning her bachelor's degree. She and her family defined their success criteria, understood their boundaries, and were willing to think beyond a two-hundred-mile radius of home.

Not every student has the credentials to earn scholarship dollars from the schools he or she wants to attend. Students need to select schools where they are considered to be above average. Community colleges, junior colleges, and state universities are terrific options for kids who are average or slightly below-average students. Again, it's the theory of relativity at work. Students should look for a place that fits their credentials and that their family can afford.

Case Study: University of Alabama[31]

Ronald Nelson is a student made famous for attending the University of Alabama. He applied to and was accepted by all eight Ivy League schools, which is a remarkable accomplishment by itself. The University of Alabama caught wind of him and offered him a free ride for all four years. None of the Ivies offered him a dime, so he chose Alabama. This kid was smart enough to get into every Ivy League school, and he chose Alabama to graduate with a debt-free degree.

ATHLETIC SCHOLARSHIPS

We can't talk about scholarships without addressing the unique aspects of athletic scholarships, likely the most well-known, but also misunderstood, types of scholarships available. They fall under the institutional category, and I like to call them the "play to pay" option.

Revenue sports – like men's football and basketball and nearly any sport that is televised with endorsements and media contracts – mean big scholarship money. Nonrevenue sports – golf, rowing, soccer to name a few – appreciate the generosity of the revenue sports that support their teams but understand that

---

[31]   Peter Jacobs, "Kid Who Got into Every Ivy League School Is Going to the University of Alabama—and It's a Brilliant Decision," *Business Insider*, May 14, 2015 (http://www.businessinsider.com/ronald-nelson-turned-down-every-ivy-league-school-for-university-of-alabama-2015-5).

there will be less scholarship money to spread around. With only 2 percent of high school athletes being on the receiving end of merit-based aid tied to sports, the odds are not in our favor.

Most college coaches are not sophisticated recruiters with lucrative travel budgets that allow them to find a needle in a haystack. They need our help to keep them organized (most of them aren't). We can help by making sure our student athlete stays top of mind so coaches will think of our kid when looking to fill a spot on the roster. Too many parents assume the club coach or the high school coach is promoting our star athlete. We think because we spend the money for travel teams and year-round play, our efforts and expenditures will lead to an athletic scholarship. However, that won't happen without a lot of help and some "push" marketing from us.

The best way to market our athlete is to support their efforts in the areas they can influence—grades and test scores. In today's world, college coaches are held accountable for graduating their student athletes, so they look at grades and academic performance on equal footing with athletic accomplishments. It's much easier for coaches to award money to high performers who can compete in the classroom as well as on the field.

Decisions about athletic scholarships[32] start as early as the sophomore year. I've met parents with ninth or tenth graders in club sports who think it's way too early to start marketing their child, but honestly, it's not. These days, and especially in women's sports, assessments and decisions take place sooner than ever. Few parents take the time or invest the dollars necessary to market their student in the best way. It requires effort, forethought, and a specific mindset.

---

[32] For more information about athletic scholarships, you can visit www.student-athleteshowcase.com.

Coaches in nonrevenue sports don't operate with the level of sophistication as those in revenue-generating sports. They simply don't have the same resources. Revenue-generating sports generate championships, sell out stadiums, and bring in a ton of money for their schools. On the other hand, sports such as swimming, tennis, track, and golf generally don't. Nonrevenue sports coaches work to fill seats and get people to come to events. They try to get boosters to kick in a little extra fundraising so they can attend tournaments, while the revenue-generating sports teams have their own tour buses, tutors, assistant coaches, and travel budgets. It's important to understand these differences, so we know how to appeal to the coaches we are targeting.

The National Collegiate Athletic Association (NCAA) imposes rigid restrictions about when coaches can approach students, and it depends on the sport. The rules are specific and enforced and designed to protect the student and minimize distraction. Nothing, however, prevents students from approaching a coach. We can initiate contact as early and as often as we care to, and we should.

As parents, we must get a handle on the landscape. We can't be seduced by the allure of athletic scholarships. For example, many coaches supplement their annual income by running summer athletic camps. In most cases, other coaches attend and watch showcase games, which is the perfect opportunity to start a relationship. Take advantage of the chance to make introductions and hand over a marketing package. That kind of initiative is what makes an immediate and lasting impression. But if our teenager receives an invitation from a college coach to attend camp, it's not the same as being recruited. Many parents and students don't appreciate the difference.

Truly competitive athletes want to play on the most competitive teams. It's significantly harder to receive athletic scholarship dollars from Division I schools than from Division II or III. Also, understand that playing sports at Division I colleges is the equivalent of a full-time job. If our student has good grades and is open to attending a smaller, liberal arts school (often Division III schools), the chances of being awarded an academic scholarship to play sports is pretty good. The overall experience will be more balanced between that of student and athlete.

When it comes to student athletes, the sport tends to drive school selection, which can be a shortsighted approach. Our athlete might desperately want to play at a certain school and work with a particular coach. This scenario often means that academic considerations take a back seat to the sports program. Again, emotions come into play here. When this happens, you're more likely to pay retail.

For example, a friend's son was a talented football player, and they had a great connection with the coaching staff at the University of Oklahoma. The son wanted to study architecture, but Oklahoma doesn't even have an architecture program. They were so excited about the football team and the dream of going pro that they tossed the son's career goals out the window. Ultimately, he didn't play pro ball and he didn't become an architect. He did, however, play on the scrimmage squad to prepare for all the conference games.

Case Study: Daniel P., Nebraska

Daniel P. is a bright kid who loves golf and wanted to go to a college with a good golf program. Both his parents are physicians, and he is a rare, self-assured kid who knew what he was looking for in a school. Wake Forest has one of the best golf programs at the collegiate level, but the University of Nebraska has a great overall sports tradition, and Nebraska wanted Daniel in its freshman class.

He visited both schools and was leaning toward Nebraska.

I received a call from his mother who said, "Daniel is stressing out about taking an AP versus an honors math class. He needs the AP class to get into Wake Forest, even though it's not his top choice." His mother's intuition was telling her he didn't need to take the AP class.

My immediate response was this: "Why put him through the unnecessary stress if he's leaning toward Nebraska and he can still play golf?"

The family, and certainly Daniel, did not need to add more pressure to this situation. My role here was to confirm what Mom already knew; so often, parents just need a sounding board and an objective point of view to allow themselves to follow their instincts.

Everyone needed to sit back and reexamine the *big picture*. Daniel took the honors math class and accepted a golf scholarship at Nebraska, resulting in an incredibly affordable college education. Mom and Dad were thrilled because their daughter was just a few years behind her brother, and it took the pressure off coming up with boatloads of money for Wake Forest.

GOVERNMENT

Chapter 8 covers a lot of the federal and state "scholarship" opportunities for financial aid. Federal grants are need based and geared toward families making less than $50,000 per year. The other category of free money offered by the federal government is the tax credit. A tax credit is not really a scholarship, but it is money for college provided by Uncle Sam.

Most families should try to take advantage of the American Opportunity Tax Credit, which is the most generous. More valuable than a deduction, a tax credit reduces your tax liability dollar for dollar. Over the course of our children's college education, this tax credit can be worth up to $10,000 per child.

The credit is limited to qualifying expenses, which include tuition, fees, and required course materials. With the cost of those expenses rising every year, qualifying is not difficult. However, you should be aware of one caveat: this credit can be used for only four years of college. With so many students taking more than four years to get a bachelor's degree, it's important for parents to understand that their student will outgrow eligibility if they take more than four years for their undergraduate education.

Also, this generosity is capped at certain income levels. For example, married couples are phased out after $180,000 in income, and single filers begin to lose benefits after $80,000. Unless Congress reauthorizes it, the American Opportunity Tax Credit is set to expire in 2018.[33]

---

[33] To receive updates about changes in tax credits related to higher education, join my email list at www.centerforcollegesolutions.com.

The Lifetime Learning Tax Credit is less robust, but it's not restricted to four years of college. It is considerably less attractive because it is limited to $2,000 per household, not per child.

Individual states offer some merit-based scholarships to keep their best and brightest students in the state. But remember, they also reach beyond their borders to diversify their student bodies and raise their rankings.

Chart 1.

Shift to Merit Aid at 4-Year Public Colleges

Chart 2.

Total Institutional Aid by Income Quartile at 4-Year Public Colleges

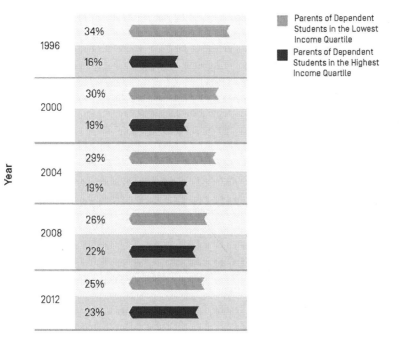

Chart 3.

Top 50 Schools by Share of Freshmen
Without Financial Need Who Receive Merit Aid

School	State	Share		Average Amount		Year	Number receiving aid	Number of freshmen
Valley City State University	ND	67.3		$1,769		2013-14	107	159
Louisiana Tech University	LA	61.7		$1,436		2012-13	783	1,289
University of North Dakota	ND	41.3		$1,173		2011-12	761	1,842
Truman State University	MO	40.5		$4,693		2012-13	508	1,254
New Mexico Tech	NM	40.5		$7,275		2013-14	128	316
University of South Carolina	SC	39.1		$5,253		2013-14	1,787	4,568
University of North Alabama	AL	36.1		$2,182		2012-13	351	971
Wichita State University	KS	36		$2,712		2012-13	438	1,215
New College of Florida	FL	35.6		$2,120		2013-14	79	222
University of Vermont	VT	33.3		$9,283		2012-13	788	2,357
Iowa State University	IA	32.6		$3,049		2012-13	1,743	5,349
Miami University	OH	31.3		$8,174		2013-14	1,139	3,637
West Virginia University	WV	30.7		$2,604		2013-14	1,510	4,913
University of Nevada-Reno	NV	30.4		$2,940		2012-13	885	2,845
Florida International University	FL	30.3		$1,080		2012-13	1,248	4,113
Ohio State University	OH	29.9		$6,757		2013-14	2,126	7,121
University of Texas at Dallas	TX	29.8		$13,766		2012-13	453	1,522
Auburn University	AL	29.6		$5,976		2012-13	1,141	3,852
University of Montana	MT	29.3		$3,250		2013-14	521	1,781
SUNY Plattsburgh	NY	28.9		$6,237		2013-14	276	953
Alcorn State University	MS	28.8		$7,190		2013-14	157	545
Mayville State University	ND	28.8		$1,307		2013-14	38	132
University of Montevallo	AL	27.9		$8,352		2013-14	145	519
Clemson University	SC	27.4		$7,456		2013-14	894	3,268

ASSESS SCHOLARSHIP OPTIONS

Continued...

School	State	Share		Average Amount		Year	Number receiving aid	Number of freshmen
U. of Alabama in Huntsville	AL	27.1		$7,494		2013-14	173	638
Oklahoma State University	OK	27		$8,291		2012-13	1,121	4,145
U. of Colorado at Boulder	CO	26.9		$9,497		2013-14	1,552	5,778
Michigan Tech. University	MI	26.7		$5,367		2013-14	334	1,252
S.D. School of Mines & Tech.	SD	26.6		$2,579		2013-14	145	546
Troy University	AL	26.5		$5,132		2013-14	428	1,613
University of Hawaii At Manoa	HI	26.1		$8,350		2012-13	441	1,687
Arizona State University	AZ	25.7		$7,733		2012-13	1,717	6,678
Colorado School of Mines	CO	25.6		$7,391		2012-13	243	949
University of Mississippi	MS	25.6		$6,876		2012-13	858	3,351
Shepherd University	WV	25.6		$9,094		2013-14	173	678
U. of Wisconsin - Oshkosh	WI	25.4		$634		2013-14	442	1,739
Dickinson State University	ND	25.1		$755		2012-13	53	211
U. of Alabama at Birmingham	AL	24.7		$8,020		2013-14	438	1,773
Minot State University	ND	24.7		$549		2012-13	87	352
SUNY College at Oneonta	NY	24.7		$2,840		2012-13	282	1,144
University of Delaware	DE	24.6		$6,074		2013-14	935	3,796
Salisbury University	MD	24.5		$2,127		2012-13	301	1,230
University of South Dakota	SD	24.5		$4,505		2012-13	306	1,250
Southern Utah University	UT	24.5		$3,863		2012-13	293	1,198
University of Alabama	AL	24.4		$11,919		2012-13	1,544	6,838
U.T. of The Permian Basin	TX	24.2		$3,132		2012-13	81	335
University of Arizona	AZ	24		$8,137		2012-13	1,672	6,955
Kansas State University	KS	24		$4,145		2012-13	910	3,786
Mississippi State University	MS	24		$3,527		2012-13	694	2,894

Chart 4.

Public Flagship Universities, by Share of Freshmen
Without Financial Need Who Receive Merit Aid

School	Share	Average Amount	Year	Number receiving aid	Number of freshmen
University of North Dakota	41.3	$1,173	2011-12	761	1,842
University of South Carolina	39.1	$5,253	2013-14	1,787	4,588
University of Vermont	33.3	$9,408	2012-13	786	2,357
West Virginia University	30.7	$2,604	2013-14	1,510	4,913
University of Nevada at Reno	30.4	$2,940	2012-13	865	2,845
• Ohio State University	29.9	$6,757	2013-14	2,126	7,121
University of Montana	29.3	$3,250	2013-14	521	1,781
University of Colorado at Boulder	28.9	$9,497	2013-14	1,552	5,778
University of Hawaii at Manoa	26.1	$9,102	2012-13	441	1,687
University of Mississippi	25.6	$6,876	2012-13	858	3,351
• University of Delaware	24.6	$6,074	2013-14	935	3,796
University of South Dakota	24.5	$4,505	2012-13	306	1,250
University of Alabama	24.4	$11,919	2012-13	1,544	6,638
University of Arizona	24	$8,137	2012-13	1,672	6,955
University of Iowa	23	$4,115	2012-13	988	4,293
University of Oklahoma	22.7	$4,540	2012-13	928	4,089
University of Kentucky	22	$7,789	2013-14	1,016	4,619
University of Missouri	21.1	$4,363	2013-14	1,277	6,060
University of Idaho	21.1	$3,133	2012-13	345	1,637
University of Maryland	19.9	$6,451	2012-13	773	3,893
University of Michigan	17.9	$4,938	2012-13	1,098	6,124
• Indiana University	17.6	$7,671	2012-13	1,333	7,579
University of Minnesota	17.4	$5,875	2013-14	965	5,538
University of Kansas	17.4	$3,235	2012-13	634	3,653

© Copyright New America & Stephen Burd. From "The Out-of-State Student Arms Race"

Continued...

School	Share		Average Amount		Year	Number receiving aid	Number of freshmen
University of Arkansas	16.3	«	$4,146	«	2013–14	703	4,300
University of Wyoming	15.4	«	$2,548	«	2012–13	243	1,578
Louisiana State University	15.2	«	$3,233	«	2012–13	867	5,717
University of Alaska at Fairbanks	15	«	$4,306	«	2012–13	114	761
University of Tennessee	13.8	«	$5,071	«	2013–14	592	4,300
University of New Hampshire	13.3	«	$8,020	««	2012–13	376	2,821
University of California at Berkeley	13	«	$4,583	«	2013–14	609	4,684
University of Maine	12.8	«	$4,030	«	2013–14	276	2,148
University of Connecticut	12.8	«	$7,045	««	2013–14	478	3,741
University of Massachusetts	11.8	«	$4,386	«	2012–13	552	4,671
University of Nebraska	11.6	«	$5,589	«	2012–13	455	3,918
U. of Illinois at Urbana-Champaign	10.9	«	$3,980	«	2011–12	753	6,914
Rutgers University	12.1	«	$4,300	«	2012–13	773	6,393
University of Rhode Island	9	«	$6,354	««	2013–14	268	2,972
Pennsylvania State University	7.8	«	$3,230	«	2012–13	590	7,605
University of Utah	7.7	«	$7,917	««	2013–14	216	2,790
University of Wisconsin at Madison	7	«	$3,989	«	2013–14	445	6,323
University of Georgia	6.9	«	$2,019	«	2013–14	359	5,211
University of Florida	5.4	‹	$2,000	«	2012–13	340	6,298
University of Oregon	5.3	‹	$5,207	«	2013–14	209	3,920
U. of North Carolina at Chapel Hill	3.2	‹	$8,393	««	2012–13	127	3,914
University at Buffalo (SUNY)	2.6	‹	$6,030	«	2012–13	93	3,614
University of Virginia	2.5	‹	$5,821	«	2013–14	89	3,516
University of Washington	2	‹	$7,000	««	2013–14	125	6,203
University of Texas at Austin	1		$5,586	«	2013–14	74	7,249

Chart 5.
Public Regional Colleges by Share of Freshmen Without Financial Need Who Receive Merit Aid

School	State	Share		Average Amount		Year	Number receiving aid	Number of freshmen
Valley City State University	ND	67.3		$1,769		2013–14	107	159
Louisiana Tech University	LA	61.7		$1,438		2012–13	783	1,289
Truman State University	MO	40.5		$4,693		2012–13	508	1,254
University of North Alabama	AL	38.1		$2,182		2012–13	351	971
Wichita State University	KS	36		$2,712		2012–13	438	1,215
Florida International University	FL	30.3		$1,080		2012–13	1,246	4,113
SUNY Plattsburgh	NY	28.9		$8,237		2013–14	276	953
Alcorn State University	MS	28.8		$7,190		2013–14	157	545
Mayville State University	ND	28.8		$1,307		2013–14	38	132
University of Montevallo	AL	27.9		$8,352		2013–14	145	519
Troy University	AL	26.5		$5,132		2013–14	428	1,613
Shepherd University	WV	25.6		$9,094		2013–14	173	676
University of Wisconsin – Oshkosh	WI	25.4		$834		2013–14	442	1,739
Dickinson State University	ND	25.1		$755		2012–13	53	211
Minot State University	ND	24.7		$549		2012–13	87	352
SUNY College at Oneonta	NY	24.7		$2,840		2012–13	282	1,144
Salisbury University	MD	24.5		$2,127		2012–13	301	1,230
Southern Utah University	UT	24.5		$3,863		2012–13	293	1,198
Bemidji State University	MN	22.5		$9,262		2013–14	122	542
University of Toledo	OH	22.4		$5,220		2013–14	751	3,229

© Copyright New America & Stephen Burd. From "The Out-of-State Student Arms Race"

Because state programs are lucrative and in short supply, deadlines matter. Many state programs are first-come first-served and use the FAFSA deadlines as their starting point. Do not dawdle. Get your submissions in as early as possible on the federal level and pay close attention to your state's deadlines for various awards. A great resource for locating the programs available in your home state is www.nasfaa.org.

PRIVATE SCHOLARSHIPS

Every year, parents ask if I can help their students find scholarship money. It's the "Where's Waldo?" exercise for finding money for college. Third party scholarship money (for example from Kiwanis Club, Coca-Cola, and utility companies) makes up 6 percent of the three-billion-dollar pie that is the total financial aid available in the US each year. That's a lot of money, but this requires the most time and effort from our students, excellent (not average) organizational and project management skills, and an incredible amount of persistence. It can be fruitful, however, be prepared to complete 50 applications to yield three scholarships.

Finding, applying to, and earning private or third-party scholarship money should be viewed as a part-time job. I recommend that students devote six to eight hours per week in their pursuit of this variety of free money. They will need some hands-on guidance and supervision because this category of scholarships is complicated.

Several credible scholarship search engines exist, but unfortunately, there is no one-stop shop. Students need to enter their personal data and identify scholarship opportunities. Because the business model for these aggregators is to sell the data captured on their "free" websites, I advise students to *set up a separate email address for all scholarship applications* and be prepared for tons of junk mail—electronic and snail mail.

Students can begin looking and applying for third-party, private scholarships as early as their sophomore year of high school. The deadlines for most of the meaningful money will be before March 1, of their senior year. This is strictly a numbers game. As I mentioned, our kids will have to complete many applications to earn few scholarships.

I don't want to discourage folks from pursuing private scholarships, but it is a rare household that does the work necessary to yield meaningful results. The ones that do the legwork usually garner several thousand dollars to offset the costs of the first year of college, however.

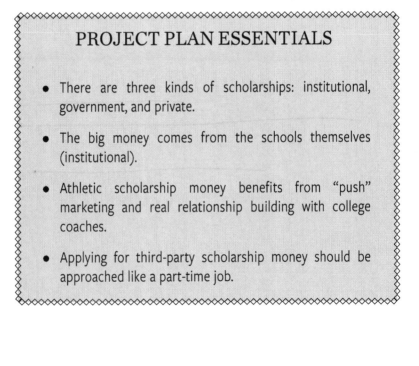

PROJECT PLAN ESSENTIALS

- There are three kinds of scholarships: institutional, government, and private.

- The big money comes from the schools themselves (institutional).

- Athletic scholarship money benefits from "push" marketing and real relationship building with college coaches.

- Applying for third-party scholarship money should be approached like a part-time job.

CHAPTER ELEVEN

COMPARE AWARD
OFFERS

James was one of those kids you have to love: personable, humble, and hardworking. Almost all the schools he had applied to offered substantial merit-based aid. Neither of his parents had gone to college, and he had two younger brothers. The whole thing was a bit overwhelming for them all.

Mom called me with a frantic tone in her voice. "He's got it in his head he needs to go to Creighton, but it looks like it's more expensive to go there than at the University of Denver."

She was right.

When the various offers were evaluated side-by-side, it would cost him $4,800 a year more to go to Creighton than the University of Denver (DU). But James really liked the vibe at Creighton, and it had a strong track record for making sure their undergrads went on to the graduate program he was keenly interested in. James was down in the dumps because his parents had made it clear he would attend a school that fit but also one that cost the least. They had two other boys to put through college, and James understood the realities of the situation.

He naïvely thought once the award letters were sent, he had to make his choice.

I explained to the family that James could share the award letter from DU with the financial aid department at Creighton. He could explain that his decision was related to finances, but if all things were equal, he preferred Creighton. He and his mother looked at me like I was from another planet. They had no idea it was possible to have this kind of conversation. As far as they knew, you get what you get, and you don't throw a fit.

I let them know that it might not work. Just because you have an impressive award from another school doesn't automatically mean a college will change what they've already offered. In James's case, an interesting thing happened.

Creighton told him to call back in three weeks. What James didn't understand at the time was that the financial aid department was waiting to see what was "coming back into inventory." The phrase refers to money the school offers to desirable students who decide to go elsewhere. The school didn't know if they'd have more money or not, so they told James to call back in a few weeks.

Three weeks later, as soon as the financial aid office opened, James and his mother called Creighton. The school was pleased to tell him they found an additional $5,000 in merit-based aid per year and would be delighted if he would accept the offer.

Will this scenario play out for everyone? No. The school has to want the student. Can a similar response be expected at every school? No. The school may have more kids accepting offers than they need. The fact is, it depends, but it's worth a shot.

If our student has done well in high school, if we have put our financial house in order, and if our family has applied to schools that view our student as a desirable addition to their incoming freshman class, colleges will create meaningful incentives for attendance. About a month prior to National Decision Day (May 1), most students receive award letters from the various colleges. Each school communicates the information differently, but they will provide a written summary of what they are prepared to offer in terms of free money, money that can be borrowed, or jobs the student can do (work study) with untaxed income that can be used to offset college costs.

An uninformed family takes those offers at face value and accepts the award outright. The recommended "never pay retail" approach is to view those initial offers as a stepping-stone. The award letter is an opportunity to reach out to the school that the student is most interested in and ask if it is willing to improve its award based on the offers made by competing schools. Obviously, if the offers from other schools are smaller, we have no leverage and cannot make a compelling argument. If, however, they are stronger, we owe it to ourselves to have the conversation.

Don't worry. This exercise is *not* the same as haggling over the price of a new car. There is a certain finesse and decorum that can work in a family's favor if we allow the strength of the offers from competing schools do the work for us. If we have a better offer from another college, we can ask a school if it is willing to meet or exceed that offer. We are asking for that the award be adjusted to match the final "net price," or out-of-pocket expense we would incur by attending that school, which is more than a fair request to make. If we're concerned about coming across as too pushy or don't know how to approach the conversation, follow this template:

Dear (name of Financial Aid Officer),

I am really excited to have received my offer of admission and aid award letter from [insert the name of the college— College A—here], and I would very much like to accept. However, I have received another offer—a better offer— from [insert the other college's name—College B—here].

Although College A is my first choice, my family cannot afford to enroll me at the current award level. Would you consider increasing my aid so that my net price is the same as College B? I am including a copy of the offer from College B for your review.

I am committed to enrolling at College A and would be heart-broken if I am not able to accept your offer of admission. If there are scholarships I can or should apply for, or any other documentation I can provide that makes it easy for you to match the offer from College B, please let me know.

I will do whatever it takes to attend College A! I will call you at [time] on [date] to follow up.

Sincerely,

Student's Name
Contact Information

If you can visit the school in person, bring a copy of the best offer received and hand it to the financial aid officer during a prearranged face-to-face meeting.

The student is responsible for communicating three things at the meeting:

1. I want to attend this school! This school is my number one choice.

2. My parents are telling me that financially, they can't support my number one choice.

3. If you can match the other school's financial offer, I can come here.

The parents are responsible for communicating three things:

1. We want our student to attend a school we can afford.

2. We want our student to attend the school she has her heart set on.

3. If you can match the better offer, we support our student enrolling here.

There is no guarantee this strategy will work, but like a runner in a five-thousand-meter race, picking up the pace during the final lap may mean standing on the podium to accept a medal. Here's a real-world example of how one family leveraged an offer to start this kind of conversation and gather all the facts before making the most informed decision.

Hi Beth,

We're so excited to share the good news—Chloe received a full ride from State U! Only the top 2 percent of applicants are awarded this level of support, so we feel very thankful.

Without seeming greedy, what are the odds this could be used to negotiate more scholarship money from the other places where she applied? We get that it's her home state school and some of the private universities may not "compete" with this offer, but Chloe spent considerable time finding and applying to those other schools. You told us she was very marketable, and it looks like you were right!

If the money were close, she'd prefer to go farther from home. Do you think it's worth the effort or are we kidding ourselves?

Thanks,

Proud Papa

After discussing Chloe's situation on the phone with her dad and using the strategy outlined earlier, I later received this follow-up from the proud papa:

Hi Beth,

Chloe received an increased offer from Private U—another $10,000, after we shared the offer from State U. She thought about it for a day or two and has decided to attend State U. I have to say we're relieved. It's her choice, and she "owns it," and we won't have to pay much for her college! You weren't kidding when you said this can be exhausting until the decision is made.

Thanks for your help throughout this process. We look forward to working with you again when our younger son, Blake, starts high school.

Thanks,

Proud Papa

In Chloe's case, she was able to make her decision based on the best offers from two entirely different schools. Her experience is a perfect example of why it is so important to appeal award money, even when it appears at first glance to be generous. If Chloe had her heart set on attending the private university, she would have been in a better position financially there. As it stood, she carefully weighed her options and made the best decision for herself and her family. When in doubt, always ask. You never know what wiggle room a school has when it comes to its offers.

PROJECT PLAN ESSENTIALS

- The first offer presented by the college may not be its best offer.

- Play the game until the decision deadline. We are best served by keeping the most interested parties in play so we can compare proposals. Think *Shark Tank*—see what the other sharks have to offer.

- Confidently and politely share the best offer with other schools the student is sincerely interested in.

- The student must take the lead in the request for consideration.

CHAPTER TWELVE

TRANSITION SUCCESSFULLY

The unthinkable happened at the 2008 Summer Olympics in Beijing. The United States didn't qualify for a medal in the men's or the women's 4 x 400 meter relay race. Neither team even made it to the final heat. Four of the world's fastest sprinters couldn't translate their individual talent into a team triumph because they bungled the baton pass. In other words, they failed to manage the transition.

Sending our kids off to college is an epic transition and requires considerable focus and preparation. It is vital that we get this transition right because of all that is at stake. The rules of the game change in ways you may not have considered once your student turns 18. We have to help them transition successfully by allowing them to be accountable for their financial life while we are present to answer questions, explain how things work, and show them how to solve problems once they appear.

Even the practical parts of the laundry list of items to think about can be a bit overwhelming:

Outfit their college living environment.

Parents and students alike may be surprised to learn there may not be as much space in a dorm room as the student is accustomed to at home. When in doubt, scale back on what you bring and be prepared for extra-long twin beds when you buy sheets and blankets (call ahead and confirm the mattress size).

Decide what goes with them and what stays at home.

What a great opportunity for learning to prioritize. "Must-haves" are different than "nice-to-haves," and this exercise can be very entertaining. A teenager's definition of "must-have" can differ dramatically from that of their parents, so have some fun with this. I recommend a staging area or another room for creating piles of "must-haves" and "nice-to-haves" so you can make decisions at a glance.

> **Make sure they know how to do laundry and how often to do it.**

Creating this habit well before dropping them on campus isn't too difficult and reduces the likelihood of pink underwear and piles of dirty laundry coming home over winter break.

> **Confirm that the room is bug free and that the mattress provided doesn't have bed bugs.**

Know what to look for.

- Inspect the room and bedding before unpacking and setting up house.

- Encase mattress, box spring, or futon in a bed bug–proof, airtight cover to keep insects out or contained.

- Store clothing and personal items in garment bags, dry cleaning bags, luggage liners, and laundry bags to keep bed bugs out.

- Keep floors clear and counter clutter to a minimum to reduce the risk of bed bugs. Regular vacuuming and frequent removal of garbage can eliminate their food sources and make a difference.

- Frequently wash clothing and bedding in warm water and tumble dry for at least thirty minutes.

- Don't bring secondhand bedding, furniture (especially if upholstered), books, or clothing home without a thorough inspection.

- Let the resident assistant (RA) or landlord know if bed bugs are suspected in or around your dorm room, apartment building, or house.

> **Pray the roommate situation is a good one or get it changed pronto.**

College roommate horror stories are all too common. Learning to live with a stranger(s) is an entirely different "education." Students learn to advocate for their needs, define boundaries, and come to terms with different lifestyles. But if it gets to the point where your student can't function, it's time to make a change. Find out how this process works before any problems arise.

> **Make sure they know how to manage money and not end up with too much month at the end of their bank balance.**

Too often, parents drop their kids off at college, and they've had *zero* experience handling their financial life because Mom or Dad have always taken care of those things. Then parents wonder why their kids can't seem to manage their money.

Like lessons in laundry, it's best to begin these while they still live under your roof. Give kids the responsibility to pay for their own gas, mobile phone bill, car insurance, clothes, and so forth, even if you still fund these lifestyle expenses for them.

Figure out what those annual expenses are and divide by 12. Then deposit the money into the student's checking account each month (like a paycheck) so they can manage the payments. To help them transition successfully, we need to allow them to be accountable for their financial life while we are there to answer questions, explain how things work, and show them how to solve the problem once it presents itself. We want our kids to make a $30 mistake, rather than a $300 error, so we can work through the problem with them and use those teachable moments to help them begin to manage money.

> **Provide your student with a low-limit credit card for use in emergencies.**

This is all about safety nets and escape hatches. A thoughtful discussion about the role a credit card can play in an emergency is important here. Paying for pizza to be delivered because the dorm food isn't so great does not constitute an emergency in most households, so we need to paint a vivid picture of what we mean by emergency.

> **Send your student off with necessary vaccinations, prescriptions, and clean teeth.**

Before we take a cross-country road trip, we make sure the car is tuned up, well oiled, and the gas tank full. We want to make sure our kids are "tuned up" and have full tanks before we drop them off too.

> Implement a strategy to protect prescription drugs from theft (a big problem on college campuses).

If your student takes prescription drugs of any kind, you need to prepare him or her for the fact that they could be stolen. Arriving on campus with a safe hiding place that only we know about is a prudent approach to make sure the meds are used as intended.

> Explain your student's health insurance plan so they understand how to access benefits on their end if the need arises.

If our child turns eighteen before heading off to school, have them go to the doctor or dentist without accompanying them. Let them get used to the administrative aspects of being an adult. When I took my son to the dermatologist at age thirteen, I handed him the new patient paperwork to fill out. He wasn't too happy about it, but by the time he goes off to college, he'll have had lots of practice.

> Teach them how to manage their diet, exercise, and sleep so they can function well and stay healthy.

Anxiety is running rampant on college campuses these days. Self-care has never been more important than it is now. Anything we can do to help our kids understand their triggers, thresholds, and boundaries so they can do what they need to do will be rewarded with better outcomes.

> **Create strategies for time management, stress management, and anxiety.**

Mindset is critical, especially during the first semester of the freshman year of college. You've laid the groundwork for the right mindset in anticipation of applying for college, but continue to support your student in this area. Tools like calmcirclecollege.com and Coach-on-Call can provide students with outlets when they become overwhelmed and don't want to admit there's a problem to Mom or Dad.

> **Schedule a weekly call, FaceTime, or Skype session.**

One way to let your student be while still having a barometer of what's going on is to have a touch-base session every week. That way, we don't have to wonder if we'll hear from them, and they don't have to feel obligated to report in on every little matter that comes up.

> **Book a room for parents' weekend before we kiss them good-bye.**

If we're planning to participate in parents' weekend, it's smart to make arrangements as soon as the dates are announced. Accommodations fill up quickly, and we'll want to make sure we can focus on enjoying our time with our newly independent student.

Most parents don't bungle these aspects of the baton pass. It's the transition from manager to mentor, participant to spectator, or spokesperson to bystander that proves the most challenging. It's as if someone flipped a switch, and we find ourselves persona non grata in an instant.

The institutions—colleges, financial aid departments, health-care facilities, and landlords—allow us to pay the bills, but they don't want to deal with us. In fact, the law prohibits them from interacting with us. The institution's relationship and allegiance is with our child. In many instances, our young adult does not quite grasp the responsibility that is laid at his or her feet overnight.

Once our kids turn 18, the world views them as an adult: They can vote, join the military, be summoned for jury duty, buy cigarettes, and sign legally binding contracts. They become entitled to the same privacy protections that adults enjoy.

The institutions that rely heavily on federal funding are paranoid about infringing on Family Educational Rights and Privacy Act (FERPA) or Health Insurance Portability and Accountability Act (HIPAA) privacy rules. Doing so *could result in the reduction or elimination of those government dollars.* Therefore, they fiercely protect the privacy of the student, sometimes beyond the scope and intent of the law, which can result in aggravation and frustration for all involved, especially parents. Don't expect anyone employed by an institution to look beyond the letter of the law or to interpret the rules in your favor.

The real-world, "well-intentioned but poorly executed" infrastructure has become a Frankenstein we all have to deal with. With a little preparation, you'll be ready to contend with any of the following situations:

- The college coach won't discuss his star point guard's injury—witnessed by twenty-five thousand screaming fans in the field house and millions more watching the TV broadcast—because he believes HIPAA prevents him from commenting.

- The mother of a 21-year-old asks to see her son's medical records, but the student doesn't want his mother to know he's been treated for a sexually transmitted disease. The college has no choice but to refuse to share the information.

- A father stands in the emergency room with his daughter who is writhing in pain from a kidney stone that appeared on their drive to freshman orientation, and the medical staff refuses to take instruction from him because the patient is eighteen.

It's important that you understand the rules you must work with, and the table on the following page will help.

	FERPA	HIPAA
Purpose	Privacy of EDUCATIONAL records	Regulates the use and disclosure of protected health information (PHI). Specifically excludes educational records protected by FERPA.
Application	Only applies to STUDENTS	Applies to everyone
Jurisdiction	Applies only when student medical records are released outside the health center and become educational records rather than treatment records.	Federal law, but bows to state law where state law is MORE stringent.
Common Sense	Have student authorize parents' access to anything governed by FERPA.	Have student authorize parents' access to anything governed by HIPAA.

We can tear our hair out in frustration and allow ourselves to become victims of government bureaucracy, or we can get busy avoiding these circumstances before they take root. We can provide invisible training wheels for the adulthood our kids are being asked to demonstrate. Let's come to terms with the legal landscape we're operating in and send our kids off to college armed with the tools necessary to handle things as they unfold.

Investing a bit of energy and effort up front by putting several legal documents in place the day we celebrate our kids' 18th birthday (or shortly thereafter) allows us to get on with life. We can enjoy the peace of mind that comes with knowing we're going into this transition as prepared as possible.

FERPA Consent to Release Student Information

TO: _____
(Name of University Official and Department that will be releasing the educational records)

Please provide information from the educational records of _____ [Name of Student requesting the release of educational records] to:

_____ [Name(s) of person to whom the educational records will be released, and if appropriate the relationship to the student such as "parents" or "prospective employer" or "attorney"]

(Note: this Consent does not cover medical records held solely by Student Health Services or the Counseling Center – contact those offices for consent forms.)

The only type of information that is to be released under this consent is:
_____ transcript
_____ disciplinary records
_____ recommendations for employment or admission to other schools
_____ all records
_____ other (specify) _____

The information is to be released for the following purpose:
_____ family communications about university experience
_____ employment
_____ admission to an educational institution
_____ other (specify)_____

    I understand the information may be released orally or in the form of copies of written records, as preferred by the requester. I have a right to inspect any written records released pursuant to this Consent (except for parents' financial records and certain letters of recommendation for which the student waived inspection rights). I understand I may revoke this Consent upon providing written notice to [Name of Person listed above as the University Official permitted to release the educational records]. I further understand that until this revocation is made, this consent shall remain in effect and my educational records will continue to be provided to [Name of Person listed above to whom the educational records will be released] for the specific purpose described above.

        Name (print)_____

        Signature_____

        Student ID Number_____

        Date_____

HIPAA Privacy Authorization Form
Authorization for Use or Disclosure of Protected Health Information
(Required by the Health Insurance Portability and Accountability Act — 45 CFR Parts 160 and 164)

1. I hereby authorize all medical service sources and health care providers to use and/or disclose the protected health information ("PHI") described below to my agent identified in my durable power of attorney for health care named _____.

2. Authorization for release of PHI covering the period of health care (check one)
    a.   ☐ from (date) _____ - to (date)_____ OR
    b   ☐ all past, present and future periods.

3. I hereby authorize the release of PHI as follows (check one):
    a.   ☐ my complete health record (including records relating to mental health care, communicable diseases, HIV or AIDS, and treatment of alcohol/drug abuse). OR
    b.   ☐ my complete health record *with the exception of the following information* (check as appropriate):
    ☐ Mental health records
    ☐ Communicable diseases (including HIV and AIDS)
    ☐ Alcohol/drug abuse treatment
    ☐ Other (please specify): _____ .

4. In addition to the authorization for release of my PHI described in paragraphs 3 a and 3 b of this Authorization, I authorize disclosure of information regarding my billing, condition, treatment and prognosis to the following individual(s):

Name _____ Relationship _____

Name _____ Relationship _____

Name _____ Relationship _____

5. This medical information may be used by the persons I authorize to receive this information for medical treatment or consultation, billing or claims payment, or other purposes as I may direct.

6. This authorization shall be in force and effect until nine (9) months after my death or _____, (date or event) at which time this authorization expires.

7. I understand that I have the right to revoke this authorization, in writing, at any time. I understand that a revocation is not effective to the extent that any person or entity has already acted in reliance on my authorization or if my authorization was obtained as a condition of obtaining insurance coverage and the insurer has a legal right to contest a claim.

8. I understand that my treatment, payment, enrollment, or eligibility for benefits will not be conditioned on whether I sign this authorization.

9. I understand that information used or disclosed pursuant to this authorization may be disclosed by the recipient and may no longer be protected by federal or state law.

_____   Date: _____
Signature of Patient

Keep original, and give copies to your health care provider, agent and family members

A final word to the wise: I've come to appreciate the benefit of redundant record systems in our increasingly complicated world. I recommend everyone (student, parents, institutions) have a copy of important documents, financial information, and the corresponding user IDs and passwords that relate to online access to accounts. At a minimum, you'll want to start with the following:

- Driver's license

- Student ID

- Birth certificate

- Social Security card

- Passport

- Health insurance card

- Bank accounts

- Credit cards

- Utilities (recent statements listing account and customer service numbers)

- Vehicle documents (title, registration, insurance)

- Electronic device details and access (smartphone, computer, tablet)

- Social media access (user name and password at a minimum)

- Email account(s)

- Emergency contact information (should be listed in CONTACTS on your phone under ICE–stands for **In Case of Emergency** and first responders know to look for this and how to access)

- Power of attorney (health care and financial recommended)

- Living will or advance directives

Every family should also have a digital copy (or additional hard copies in separate and safe location) of important documents that can be easily accessed if the original copies are misplaced. Students typically change residences several times during the college years, so the chance for something important to go missing borders on inevitable. I'd hate to see a family go to all this effort only to realize when they needed their documents most, they can't get their hands on them.[34]

A Properly Managed College Project in the Real World

Every so often, you get lucky. Fred Astaire was partnered with Ginger Rogers. Batman had Robin. Luke found Obi-wan Kenobi. Sometimes things just click and work the way they are supposed to.

That's been my experience with the Drosendahl family.

The fact is, they did all the real work of preparing for their college project before we met. Because they embody my project

---

[34] Our clients are automatically enrolled in a digital vault that allows them to store everything in an encrypted, secure location that is accessible to trusted individuals only they authorize.

plan philosophy more than any other family I've had the privilege of working with, I'll share their feedback with you here. They are an example of a family who understands everyone's roles and responsibilities during the process and executes efficiently. Their firsthand account illustrates some real-world applications of the advice, tips, and insights I've shared in the preceding chapters. My hope is you'll see that you, too, can plan and prepare for college accordingly.

FROM MATTHEW AND BETHANY DROSENDAHL

Drosendahl & Drosendahl Inc.: producing high-quality human beings since 1995

NEVER PAY RETAIL FOR COLLEGE.

That is excellent advice! Having successfully sent two students to college (NOT paying retail!) and being well on our way to sending the third and final, here are our thoughts on what parents should do when sending kids to college:

Take the long view.

Ideally, this journey starts when you pick your partner. Matthew and I are accountants, so we have always had a plan. If your family isn't that detail oriented, make a point of starting this process the summer before your student's freshman year of high school. There is a bit of a formula to building a young person's college résumé.

- Freshman year: If your student doesn't already have an established activity, have him or her sample activities and pick the two that he or she enjoys the most.

- Sophomore year: Focus on an activity that he or she is interested in. Find a place for your student to volunteer.

- Junior year: Create a job or business opportunity from relationships at school or volunteer work.

- Senior year: Keep your eye on the prize and finish strong. If you start a little later, no worries.

There is no one perfect fit, so take the accumulation of your student's accomplishments and dress it up. Other examples of thinking long term include making your student responsible for checking his or her own grades; you are there only to help facilitate *his* or *her* goals; your student should know how to clean his or her bedroom, bathroom and do laundry (have him or her choose a laundry day); practice what you want them to be successful at.

Determine your family goals and set appropriate expectations.

For our family, the goals were simple: in high school, grades matter; school is considered complete with at least a four-year degree. The expectations for college: you graduate college with marketable skills (*No* barista degrees!); you graduate college with *no* debt; you have $100,000 to spend. If you can figure out a way to pay for college and your expenses, the extra money is yours! From early on, we talked to our children about the opportunities they have. It was up to them to take the actions required to take advantage of those opportunities. We were their helpers, their coaches, their administrative assistants, and their cheerleaders. And yes, there were moments of upset, tears, debate, eye-rolling, and adjustment (the kids had a few special moments as well).

Understand who your student is.

What motivates your student? What is your student's strength? Where would your student require additional support or skills? The goal is to maximize your student's strengths and develop healthy habits, new skills, and support for softer areas. Wherever your student goes to college (and high school) needs to be a good fit for him or her.

Understand where the opportunities are.

College is a business, and the market is full of all different types of institutions that provide a wide variety of services. By taking some time to understand the different types of schools, you can begin to see various opportunities for your student and family.

Recognize that there are different paths to the same end goal.

I was saddened to have lost a friendship with a friend over a discussion regarding her daughter's (or should I say the parents') chosen college path. They had her apply to only Ivy League schools. This young lady is a great kid, but it was unlikely she would be accepted by an Ivy League school. (And don't even get me started about the return on investment.) By the end of December of her senior year, she had not been accepted to any colleges. While her friends were happily and busily deciding which school they would attend and adding up all the scholarships they had earned, she was starting the application process all over. In addition, she missed opportunities with great institutions that could have eventually led her to the Ivy Leagues. All of this is to say, don't overlook the benefits of accredited junior or community colleges and local college intuitions. If your student plans on earning a degree higher than a bachelor's, it doesn't matter where his or her first degree is from. Save your money on the first degree and go to the big-name school for your second degree. Be smart, be strategic, and be realistic.

When everyone zigs, you can zag.

As parents, we want the best for our children. We worry and become overwhelmed. Things change. Sometimes we just don't know what to do or how to do it. In these moments, it is great to ask for help *and* to understand that it is *not* a one-size-fits-all world. There are endless opportunities for every student. One big red flag for me is when people say, "always" or "never." I find that always and never rarely applies in life.

Yes, there is important information to pay attention to like deadlines and specific requirements. But when someone starts telling you or your student things like, "You won't get into college if you take two study halls" or "You have to take this test" or "You need to have XX hours of volunteer hours," just smile, say, "Thanks for the information." Then walk away. Don't let fear drive you into a herd mentality. Your student may need two study halls to be successful. Some colleges *don't* require standardized tests. Mastering one great skill is far more valuable than a thousand hours of patchwork busyness.

Take the long view and enjoy the journey because, ten years after college, no one asks where you graduated from.

A Successful College Project Plan – in the Real World

MADDY:

University of Denver, CO, mechanical engineering,
Chancellor's Scholarship

JACQUELYN:

University of Denver, CO, Daniels College of Business,
Chancellor's Scholarship

JONATHAN:

Entering early college as a junior in high school, University
of Colorado, Colorado Springs and Pikes Peak Community
College; potential future major—computer, mechanical, or
aerospace engineering

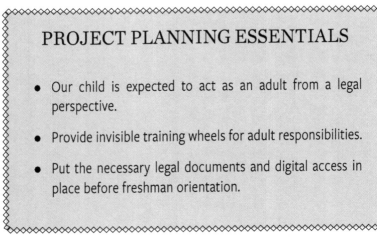

PROJECT PLANNING ESSENTIALS

- Our child is expected to act as an adult from a legal perspective.

- Provide invisible training wheels for adult responsibilities.

- Put the necessary legal documents and digital access in place before freshman orientation.

CONCLUSION

I f the only outcome we wanted for our kids from the project called college was a job, we might be better off taking our six-figure investment and buying them a franchise.

Seriously.

Why not align them with a proven business model, structured training, and a path toward a steady paycheck? Turns out, there are a lot of similarities in vetting a franchise and sending our kids to college.

When determining whether to become a franchisee, there is an amalgamated list[35] of tips you will find within twenty minutes of online research:

1. Understand your personality type and assess your strengths.

2. Research the franchise models that seem like a good fit for your background, interests, and experiences.

3. Make sure you have the financial resources to support yourself while you're building your business—beyond the initial licensing fees and start-up costs. It will probably take twice as long and cost twice as much as the brochures suggest.

4. Look beyond the marketing hype and talk to at least half a dozen other franchise owners about their experience.

5. Use a board of advisers to guide you in your decision making (accountant, lawyer, business coach, banker, etc.).

6. Visit several franchise locations and work in the environment before signing on the dotted line.

7. Understand the rules.

8. Create a game plan and work it.

35   Susan Adams, "12 Things to Do before You Buy a Franchise," *Forbes*, June 22, 2016 (http://www.forbes.com/sites/susanadams/2016/06/22/12-things-to-do-before-you-buy-a-franchise/#2edaaf396527).

9. Twenty percent of franchises thrive because the licensees understand the model is their starting point, not their end game.

10. Eighty percent of franchisees barely make it because they expect the business to come to them.

For most of us, college for our kids is not simply a path toward their eventual employment. The expectations rolled up into the college project plan are so much more.

In my years of working with parents, here's what I've learned most parents want for their children from the college experience:

- An opportunity to hold themselves capable and accountable for decisions they're making and actions they're taking.

- A place where they can explore their beliefs and measure them against peers with differing points of view.

- A petri dish for interacting with new people, broadening their boundaries, and developing an expanded worldview.

- A "raising of the bar" in terms of expectations and performance.

- A spark to the pilot light that inspires them to take action.

- An environment where they can continue to chisel away at their block of marble and reveal more of themselves to themselves.

- And, oh, by the way, some marketable skills that get them off our payroll after graduation.

What makes college such a unique project is the emotional capital—in addition to the financial resources—required of us as a family. The financial investment is significant, increasing, and challenging on a good day. But that part of this equation pales in comparison to the emotional investment we're making. We can't care less or set our emotions aside in this process. These are our kids.

We can think and act differently, balancing the intensity of our emotions with the responsibilities of getting the job done and done right.

Many parents become overwhelmed or paralyzed with the magnitude of the challenge college poses. But if we (1) break it down into manageable pieces, (2) approach it as the multiyear project plan it is, (3) allow our student to take care of his or her end of the bargain, (4) take care of what we as parents must do, and (5) then meet in the middle on those things that require us to work together, we can avoid paying retail for college. The Project Plan Essentials at the end of each chapter can serve as a reminder of what to focus on for each segment of the project.

I started down this path for admittedly self-serving reasons. Finding a way to minimize the investment we would make in Mack's college education was my primary motive for exploring this thing called "college planning." I could not have known where it would lead, and I am humbled by what I've learned along the way and the families that have allowed me to collaborate with them. I'm thankful every day for having chosen this path because it has shaped my perspective both personally and professionally.

I've come to appreciate the fact that we cannot accomplish the project called college alone or with just a little help. To do it right, it takes the efforts of subject matter experts who coach, guide, inform, and advise at the appropriate stage of the project. Once I understood that I couldn't possibly provide all the solutions a family needed to create the best outcome for their situation and realized my role was to find the resources that could, things began to fall into place. When a problem-solver realizes they have to go find a better and different problem-solver, it's a game changer. On one hand, it's a relief to understand you can't know everything; on the other hand, it's an inspiring challenge to find the resources that can make a difference for a family. That kind of matchmaking yields some incredible magic.

How does this team work, and how do we achieve the best possible outcome when it comes to college? Simple. We approach it like a six-figure kitchen remodel.

A project of this scope requires a variety of subcontracted experts to come together in a sequence of success that brings it in on time and on budget. I think the real "ah-ha" moment for me was understanding that the student manages some of the project components, the parent(s) manages some of the project components, and then both parent and student have to come together and collaborate on some of the project components. Finally, there is a need for a senior project manager—someone who is not emotionally involved in the outcome—that is responsible for the *big* picture. And that senior project manager needs to direct the parents and student, when it makes sense, to pay for help getting critical parts of the project completed.

College is a project plan that entails a significant number of moving parts with a defined deadline. The process of applying for admission and financial aid has grown so big and complex, and the stakes so high personally and financially, we parents need help. We need it in the form of information: high quality, filtered for relevance to our circumstances, in digestible amounts. Parents also need guidance and caring support from people whose loyalty is not split. Involving the perspective and expertise of professionals that have spent years learning how to find a solution in a matter of hours is worth its weight in gold. Most families will attempt the college project two or three times; benefitting from the experience of those that do it dozens or hundreds of times a year offers a return on investment that is literally priceless (less time, less stress, less money).

In today's world, we have a team of professionals that help bring our child into the world, a monumental transition, for sure. We're not used to seeing the transition into adulthood the same way, but it is the birth of an adult, and college is the place where much of this happens. If we don't find support, the process can be lonely, stressful, and frustrating. When we allow caring experts in the field to help us, we have more time and energy to focus on the relationship, to be the parent we want to be, and enjoy the process of watching and guiding our children on their path.

Isn't that how we'd rather spend our time?

None of this was necessary nor even conceivable when we went to college. But our moms didn't email the school to tell them we were home sick or look up our grades on Infinite Campus, either. And we didn't upload our homework to Google Classroom or bone up on quadratic equations by viewing a YouTube video or answer questions by clicking a button instead of raising our hands … it is indeed a different world. Choosing not to adapt would be like refusing to pick up that smart phone for the very first time. Have faith. We can do this.

And the management principles and component tools for your college project are at your fingertips. This book is designed to provide you with the information, steps, and resources you need to manage the project yourself. But if any of this begins to feel overwhelming, if confusion, frustration, or anxiety threaten to make an appearance, just visit us at www. CenterForCollegeSolutions.com. We have several helpful checklists, a monthly newsletter we'd love to share, and even the opportunity for a complimentary consultation to help you focus on those things that will make a difference for your household.

I spend my days as a senior project manager for college projects all over the country. Some families just need a good blueprint that they can manage once we've talked through the details; others want to not only be held accountable for their parts of the project, but want to find the subcontractors who can guide them in areas they lack experience or confidence. Either way, our role is to connect you with the resources you need. I said in the introduction that I'm a mom on a mission. Together, we can prove that Tom Cruise isn't the only one that can do the impossible!

ADDITIONAL
RESOURCES

Chapter 2: Understand College Options

Bruni, Frank, *Where You Go Is Not Who You'll Be: An Antidote to the College Admissions Mania.*

Wagner, Tony, and Dintersmith, Ted, *Most Likely to Succeed: Preparing Our Kids for the Innovation Era.*

Chapter 3: Prep for College Admissions

College Visits:

http://blog.prepscholar.com/good-questions-to-ask-on-a-college-tour

https://bigfuture.collegeboard.org/get-started/know-yourself/6-steps-to-get-the-most-out-of-a-campus-visit

http://www.princetonreview.com/college-advice/college-visits

https://www.collegeraptor.com/college-guide/college-search/13-ways-to-make-the-most-of-your-college-visit/

http://www.thecollegesolution.com/12-questions-to-ask-about-a-colleges-disability-services/

College Essays:

Gelb, Alan, *Conquering the College Admissions Essay in 10 Steps.*

http://college.usatoday.com/2014/10/23/9-essay-writing-tips-to-wow-college-admissions-officers/

https://apply.jhu.edu/apply/essays-that-worked/

http://www.nacacnet.org/studentinfo/articles/pages/top-ten-tips-for-writing-a-college-essay-.aspx

http://www.usnews.com/education/best-colleges/articles/2014/09/30/video-learn-how-to-write-a-great-college-application-essay

College Admissions Applications:

http://www.commonapp.org/

http://www.nacacnet.org/studentinfo/breakdown/Pages/default.
aspx

https://www.unigo.com/get-to-college/college-admissions/
parents-how-to-manage-the-stress-of-the-college-application-
process

http://www.usnews.com/education/blogs/college-admissions-
playbook/2013/09/02/college-students-share-tips-for-manag
ing-the-application-process

http://collegeappwizard.com/

Test Prep Resources:

http://www.studentscholarshipsearch.com/tips/college-test-prep.php

http://www.sparknotes.com/testprep/

https://www.prepfactory.com/

https://www.number2.com/index.cfm?s=0

https://www.collegeboard.org/

http://www.act.org/

Chapter 4: Gain Self-Awareness

Cohen, Harlan, *The Naked Roommate: And 107 Other Issues You Might Run into in College.*

Hoefle, Vicki, and Kajitani, Alex, *Duct Tape Parenting: A Less Is More Approach to Raising Respectful, Responsible and Resilient Kids.*

Miller, John, *Parenting the QBQ Way: How to Be an Outstanding Parent and Raise Great Kids Using the Power of Personal Accountability.*

Pavlina, Steve, *Personal Development for Smart People: The Conscious Pursuit of Personal Growth.*

Quindlen, Anna, *A Short Guide to a Happy Life.*

Robinson, Ken, *The Element: How Finding Your Passion Changes Everything.*

Tieger, Paul, and Barron-Tieger, Barbara, *Do What You Are: Discover the Perfect Career for You through the Secrets of Personality Type.*

Todd, Henry, *Louder than Words: Harness the Power of Your Authentic Voice.*

Chapter 5: Get the Right Mindset

Ballantyne, Craig, *The Perfect Day Formula: How to Own the Day and Control Your Life.*

Brooke, David, *The Road to Character.*

Goins, Jeff, *The Art of Work: A Proven Path to Discovering What You Were Meant to Do.*

Hyatt, Michael, and Harkavy, Daniel, *Living Forward: A Proven Plan to Stop Drifting and Get the Life You Want.*

Johnson, Steven, *Where Good Ideas Come From: The Natural History of Innovation.*

Lopez, Shane. "Not Enough Students Are Success Ready," *Gallop*, April 10, 2014 (http://www.gallup.com/businessjournal/168242/not-enough-students-success-ready.aspx).

Roberts, Andrew, *The Thinking Student's Guide to College.*

Chapter 7: Apply for Financial Aid

Chany, Kalman, *Paying for College without Going Broke*

http://www.finaid.org/

https://studentaid.ed.gov/sa/

How to obtain the FAFSA Guide, Evisors:

https://www.edvisors.com/fafsa/book/user-info/

https://fafsa.ed.gov/

Everything you want to know about the CSS Profile:

https://student.collegeboard.org/css-financial-aid-profile

Chapter 9: Select Right-Fit Colleges

The College Board, *Book of Majors.*

Fiske, Edward B., *The Fiske Guide to Colleges.*

Loveland, Elaina, *Creative Colleges: A Guide for Student Actors, Artists, Dancers, Musicians and Writers.*

Lythcott-Harris, Julie, *How to Raise an Adult: Break Free of the Overparenting Trap and Prepare Your Kids for Success.*

Marthers, Janet, and Marthers, Paul, *Follow Your Interests to Find the Right College.*

Orr, Tamra B., *America's Best Colleges for B Students: A College Guide for Students without Straight A's.*

Palladino, John, *Finding the College That's Right for You.*

Pearson, Taylor, *The End of Jobs: Money, Meaning and Freedom without the 9–5.*

Pope, Loren, *Colleges That Change Lives: 40 Schools That Will Change the Way You Think about Colleges.*

Pope, Loren, *Looking beyond the Ivy League: Finding the College That's Right for You.*

The Princeton Review, *The K & W Guide to Colleges for Students with Learning Differences.*

Rugg, Frederick E., *Rugg's Recommendations on the Colleges.*

Springer, Sally, Reider, John, and Morgan, Joyce, *Admission Matters: What Parents and Students Need to Know about Getting into College.*

How to find schools:

https://collegescorecard.ed.gov/

http://www.princetonreview.com/college-rankings?rankings=best-381-colleges

http://www.schoold.co/

http://www.thecollegesolution.com/

http://nsse.indiana.edu/html/pocket_guide_intro.cfm

How to find occupations:

https://www.onetonline.org/

http://www.payscale.com/

How many students received merit-based aid from a particular college:

 http://collegedata.com/

What percentage of students received a discount on the total cost of attendance:

http://nces.ed.gov/collegenavigator/

Four-year graduation rates for each college:

http://collegeresults.org/SEE

Information on the most and least expensive state schools:

http://collegecost.ed.gov/catc/

Chapter 10: Assess Scholarship Options

http://www.mykidscollegechoice.com/full-scholarship-list/

https://bigfuture.collegeboard.org/scholarship-search

https://www.salliemae.com/plan-for-college/scholarships/

https://www.cappex.com/

https://www.petersons.com/college-search/scholarship-search.aspx

https://www.scholarships.com/

http://www.fastweb.com/

http://scholarshipstats.com/

http://student-athleteshowcase.com/home

https://store.collegeboard.org/sto/productdetail.do?Itemkey=107768

Chapter 12: Transition Successfully

Coburn, Karen Levin, and Treeger, Madge Lawrence, *Letting Go: A Parent's Guide to Understanding the College Years.*

Hoefle, Vicki, *Straight Talk on Parenting: A No-Nonsense Approach on How to Grow a Grown-Up.*

Hoefle, Vicki, and Kajitani, Alex, *Duct Tape Parenting: A Less Is More Approach to Raising Respectful, Responsible and Resilient Kids.*

Stelien, Hélène Tragos, *Moving to College: What to Do, What to Learn, What to Pack.*

Parent Resources:

https://www.universityparent.com/

http://grownandflown.com/

Mental and physical need of college students:

www.CalmCircleCollege.com

College match tools:

http://nces.ed.gov/collegenavigator/

https://www.naviance.com/

https://bigfuture.collegeboard.org/

✗ http://www.collegexpress.com/

✗ http://www.collegedata.com/cs/search/college/college_search_
tmpl.jhtml

http://www.collegeconfidential.com/college_search/

✗ https://www.collegeraptor.com/Scenario/StartCollegeSearch

ACKNOWLEDGMENTS

What I know to be true about how money *really* works I owe to Don Blanton. As the brilliant mind behind MoneyTrax (http://www.moneytrax.com/), Don has had a profound impact on the lives of so many people. The advisers who license his tools and invest in his training will change the lives of their clients, their clients' children, and their clients' children's children forever. Don's servant leadership approach and commitment to making a difference is inspiring. He has assembled an incredible team of dedicated professionals, and I thank them all for the incredible work they do.

What I've learned about comprehensive college planning is a direct result of the work of Todd Fothergill. Todd has dedicated his professional life to helping families find the right schools, for the right reasons, while paying the right price. Todd's wisdom and experience have created solutions that help families put their kids through school without going broke. Todd integrated the student and parents in his planning process before any of us understood the power of that approach and has provided a truly holistic solution for us to emulate (http://www.strategiesforcollege. com/). His intellectual property will provide the framework for The Center for College Solutions.

When I met Don and Todd, I thought, *Where have you been this whole time?* But when the student is ready, the teacher will appear. Apparently, I'm a slow learner.

What I've learned about techniques and tools that make it possible to pay for college without going broke I learned from Troy Onink. As a regular contributor to Forbes.com and the chief executive officer of Stratagee (https://www.stratagee.com/), Troy has created tools that financial advisers can use to help families understand their options and avoid paying retail for college.

What I know about financial aid and award appeals I've learned from Stuart Siegel. Stuart will forget more about all the rules, exceptions, and convoluted logic regarding financial aid than the rest of us will ever know. His expertise and friendship have kept me sane all these years. In his role as the director for the College Family Care Center and founder of College Tuition Solutions, Inc., Stuart cares about the families he serves and works tirelessly to help them achieve a better outcome. He is the one who coined the acronym POOP (parent-out-of-pocket) Score and has been gracious enough to share it with me.

What I've learned about the student side of this equation I've learned from Lisa Marker-Robbins. Lisa is a senior certified Birkman consultant, successful business owner (the founder and president of LEAP), mom, and good friend. She's artfully adapted Fortune 500 tools for everyday folks and has helped kids all over the country find their path. The world is a better place because of her.

What I've come to appreciate about mindset and the role it plays in helping kids succeed in college has come from Charmas Lee (CharmasLee.com). I grew up in an athletic household, attended college on an athletic scholarship, and have been coached by some pretty talented people. Charmas Lee is the best coach I've ever encountered, and his "Think. Say. Do." approach to creating champions—in all walks of life—is something we all need. He ignites the heart and influences the mind of every life he touches.

What I know to be true about marketing student athletes to college coaches has been brought to life by Rex Grayner. Rex is the cofounder of Student Athlete Showcase (http://student-athleteshowcase.com/home). His personal journey and commitment to helping kids connect with college coaches the right way and for the right reasons distinguishes him and his organization in a crowded field. I smile when I think of all the happy kids, satisfied coaches, and relieved parents he supports through his work.

What I know about being a professional problem solver for families during the college years I've learned from Beatrice Schultz (WestfaceCollegePlanning.com) and Kate Seastone (SimplicitFinancial.com). Their clients are fortunate to have such competent and caring advisers in their lives. Beatrice and Kate have served parents with college-bound students for years and allow me to participate in a mastermind group we formed after an industry conference several years back. When you spend time with people who are a lot smarter than you are, a few things are bound to rub off.

What it takes to be the author of a book is quite involved. But if you're open to the possibilities, you meet some truly amazing people along the way. Barri Segal got the ball rolling and passed the baton to Brooke White, who stepped in and worked tirelessly to bring some necessary structure to my madness. Thank you, ladies, for laying the foundation for this book.

A chance phone conversation with Honorée Corder, however, changed the trajectory of my life. She is the goddess of all things "book" and simply knows what needs to happen, who needs to help, and how to get stuff done. You know you have a real friend when you can pick up where you left off, even if it's been months or years since you last spoke. Honorée is that kind of friend to me and, for that, I count my blessings every day. Honorée introduced me to Leslie Watts, and I can say without hesitation she is a "word whisperer," bringing literal magic to the process of birthing a book.

I would be remiss if I failed to acknowledge that I've had the privilege of growing and learning and sharing this journey only because of the people that made it possible.

Diana Spencer was the first to let me peek behind the curtain. She gave me permission to explore a larger scope of service for the families we serve. Then Kim Kirschner came along and took it to a whole new level, pulling me up to a vantage point that introduced a brighter, broader horizon, allowing me to expand the vision far beyond my limited point of view at the time. She may never fully comprehend her influence on my world.

Enter Kate Marks. In a complete leap of faith, she picked up stakes in Minnesota and moved to Colorado based on a few great phone conversations and the Birkman Assessment's confirmation that we would work very well together. I cannot do what I do every day without her. My guardian angel works overtime and sending Kate my way is proof positive of that fact.

Jodi Lynn has been an unexpected delight. When a random resume found its way to my inbox, I suspected she was way too qualified to wander into my world, let alone invest her time and expertise in it. Her ability for thinking outside the box and my persistence in asking her to create a role she could own has made great things happen. She is a world-class integrator, and I delight in finding another Midwestern mentality that simply gets it.

Cheryl Constantino has been in my life since before Mack was born, and she's remained a loyal and calming influence on the financial planning side of my professional life every step of the way—I am forever grateful. Barclay Callender makes both Cheryl and I look smart and has managed to find a way to do whatever was needed, even when we weren't sure what that might be. Again, thanks for hanging in there with us.

Finally, a hug and a kiss and an eternal blanket of gratitude for my husband, Derek. His willingness to continue to support my "nonprofit" all these years is testament to the fact that he's a true romantic trapped in the deceiving persona of a logical engineer. I fell in love with that squishy core he so fiercely protects and thank my lucky stars we struck up a conversation on that UNITED flight from Vancouver to Chicago back in the day. Without Derek, there is no Mack. Without Mack, I would've missed this journey, and I'm having way too much fun to imagine it any other way.

WHO IS BETH WALKER?

BETH'S most important role is being the mother of a high school student, Mack. He is the reason she is on a mission to help fix the broken system of paying for college in America.

She believes we are all born with unlimited potential and our life's work is to tap it, unleash it, and reveal it. In doing so, we will fulfill our purpose in life.

Beth's purpose is all about a better future - for our children, for parents and for our communities. That's why she believes in approaching college with a project management mentality. It's something that impacts a lot of people over time.

As a scholarship athlete for the women's volleyball team at the University of Kansas, Beth earned distinction as an Academic All-American. After completing her bachelor's degree, she went to work for several large corporations including Procter & Gamble, Clorox and McKesson, moving quickly through the management ranks.

In 1999, she left the corporate world and became a financial planner. She chose this profession because she wants to be a catalyst for abundance and eliminate the scarcity mentality that many people experience around money. By alleviating financial uncertainty in clients' lives, she allows them to focus on their unique contribution.

As a Certified College Planning Specialist (CCPS), Beth is trained in the complex strategies suitable for reducing a family's out-of-pocket college expenses, routinely saving families 25%-50% on the cost of college.

She is the author of two books, An Employee's Guide to Stock Options (McGraw-Hill, 2003) and Never Pay Retail for College (Prussian Press, 2017). Beth has been quoted frequently in the press including in the Wall Street Journal, US News & World Report, CNN Money, and the Denver Post.

In 2016, she launched the Center for College Solutions, a collaborative coalition of professionals (education consultants, admissions committee members, athletic marketing experts, financial aid gurus, etc.) committed to making college an affordable reality for all families.

When she wakes in the morning, Beth is genuinely excited about what can get done that day. She's thankful for the opportunity to make something good happen. Her sense of urgency is simply because there is so much possibility.

She believes that behaving well and doing the right thing over the long haul is rewarded and we can feel child-like joy and delight as a result of being the best version of ourselves.

Beth@CenterforCollegeSolutions.com

95359601R00130

Made in the USA
Lexington, KY
08 August 2018